ALEXANDER GOEHR
COMPOSING A LIFE

**Alexander ("Sandy") Goehr** is a British composer and Emeritus Professor of Music at Cambridge University. He was born into a Jewish musical family in Berlin in 1932. His father, Walter Goehr, was a composer and conductor, and a pupil of Arnold Schoenberg. His mother, Laelia, trained as a pianist at the Kyiv Conservatory.

Goehr moved to England in 1933 when his father accepted a position as conductor there in the wake of Hitler coming to power. He was educated in Britain and spent the war in Buckinghamshire. At the Royal College of Music in Manchester, where he attended Richard Hall's classes, he formed the "Manchester School," a group of young composers and musicians—including Peter Maxwell Davies, Harrison Birtwistle, and pianist John Ogdon—who specialized in the performance of new music.

He was introduced to Olivier Messiaen's music when his father conducted the first British performance of *Turangalîla* in 1953. He subsequently went to study with Messiaen in Paris, and attended the Darmstadt Festival courses where he met and made friends with many composers, including Pierre Boulez and Luigi Nono.

He came to prominence in England in the late 1950s and early 1960s as a radical exponent of serial music. Since then, he has composed more than one hundred major works, including operas, orchestral and chamber pieces, and music for film, television, dance, and theatre.

Goehr is one of Europe's most important music educators. He was a lecturer at Southampton University, Professor of Music at Leeds University and finally the Professor of Music at Cambridge University for more than twenty-five years. He has taught many successful composers, theorists, and musicologists. Over the course of his life he has written and lectured extensively, and his works are performed all over the world. His music is published by Schott.

**Jack Van Zandt** (b. 1954) is a Grammy-winning composer of music for concerts, film and TV, and a music educator, based in Los Angeles and Ireland. He is a former pupil, as well as musical and teaching assistant to Alexander Goehr, having studied and worked with him in Cambridge between 1976 and 1985. He was recently a music faculty member at the University of Colorado, Colorado Springs, and California Institute for the Arts (CalArts). He is a new music concert producer in Los Angeles, and a founder and co-director of the Beyond Opera Collective. Van Zandt also worked as a U.S. and Irish trade book publisher in the 1990s, and is a published professional music, arts and political op-ed writer, and journalist. His music is published by Composers Edition in Oxford, U.K.

More information:
https://www.jackvanzandt.com
https://composersedition.com/jack-van-zandt/

**Sally Groves** worked in music publishing from 1970 to 2014, mainly with Schott Music, where she was Creative Director in London for many years. She has always served on musical boards and trusts. She currently chairs Opera Ventures, the Vaughan Williams Foundation, and the Music Libraries Trust, is a governor of the Royal Society of Musicians, and a trustee of the Michael Tippett Musical Foundation and the Peter Maxwell Davies Trust, as well as of various ensembles. She was awarded an MBE for services in music in 2016.

# Alexander Goehr
# *Composing a Life:*
# *Teachers, Mentors, and Models*

*Edited and with Preface, Introduction, and Commentary by*

JACK VAN ZANDT

*Foreword by*

SALLY GROVES

CARCANET LIVES AND LETTERS

First published in Great Britain in 2023 by
Carcanet
Alliance House, 30 Cross Street
Manchester, M2 7AQ
www.carcanet.co.uk

Text copyright © Jack Van Zandt 2023

The right of Jack Van Zandt to be identified as the author
of this work has been asserted in accordance with the
Copyright, Design and Patents Act of 1988; all rights reserved.

A CIP catalogue record for this book is
available from the British Library.

ISBN 978 1 80017 357 6

Book design by Andrew Latimer, Carcanet
Typesetting by LiteBook Prepress Services
Printed in Great Britain by SRP Ltd, Exeter, Devon

The publisher acknowledges financial
assistance from Arts Council England.

# CONTENTS

Acknowledgements 7
List of Photographs and Credits 8
Musical Examples 9
Foreword 11
Preface 13
Introduction 19

## PART I:
## TEACHERS AND MENTORS

1. Beginnings 39
2. Richard Hall and the Royal Manchester College of Music 52
3. Olivier Messiaen, Yvonne Loriod and the Paris Conservatoire 64
4. Pierre Boulez 80
5. Darmstadt 93
6. Hanns Eisler 106
7. Alan Hacker 119
8. Schoenberg 124
9. Ulrich Siegele 135

## INTERLUDE
## THE AMERICAN EXPERIENCE

10. Wolpe, Copland, Carter, Sessions, Schuller and Babbitt 149

## PART II
## MODELS AND EXPLORATIONS

| | |
|---|---|
| 11. Modeling | 163 |
| 12. Modality | 172 |
| 13. Figured Bass and Improvisation | 188 |
| 14. Words into Music | 199 |

## CODA
## MY FATHER'S SON

| | |
|---|---|
| 15. Walter Goehr | 215 |

| | |
|---|---|
| Student Memories of Goehr as Teacher and Mentor | 225 |
| Bibliography | 234 |
| Goehr Works List | 237 |
| Goehr Discography | 246 |
| Further Information | 252 |
| Index | 253 |

**ACKNOWLEDGEMENTS**

No book of this nature is created in a vacuum, and there are many people who have assisted editorially, lent moral support, provided materials, and given us welcome advice.

First of all, we want to thank our dear friend Sally Groves for her thoughts and ideas on this book project from the very beginning, and her encouragement and advice throughout the process.

Amira Goehr has been essential to the process of creating the book and has given us the benefit of her advice and editorial ideas from the beginning.

Jeanne Schuster put her professional copyeditor skills to work on the several drafts of the manuscript, and helped us to make the transition of the text from taped discussions to written form.

Michael Schmidt and his staff at Carcanet Press have been a joy to work with, and we are thankful for their support and advice in creating the final text of the book.

We would like to express our appreciation and special thanks to our fabulous editor, Maren Meinhardt, for her diligence, dedication, keen eye, and many excellent suggestions. She was a delight to work with and the book is very much better because of her.

Thank you to Ian Mylett and his team at Schott Music Group in London, Sandy's publishers, who created the works list and discography. And we very much appreciate Dan Goren and his staff at Composers Edition, Jack's publisher, for their enthusiasm, advice and promotional efforts.

And finally, a big thank you to Southern California-based composer and music teacher, Nina Crecia, who assisted in transcribing the many hours of recorded conversations selected for this book.

## LIST OF PHOTOGRAPHS AND CREDITS

| | |
|---|---:|
| Sally Groves and Alexander Goehr. Sally Groves Collection | 10 |
| Jack Van Zandt and Alexander Goehr. Photo by Julia Crockatt | 12 |
| Jack Van Zandt. Photo by Elisa Ferarri | 16 |
| Alexander Goehr and Jack Van Zandt, 21 December 1979. Jack Van Zandt Collection | 18 |
| Alexander Goehr as a young man, 1940s. Photo by Laelia Goehr | 38 |
| Walter Goehr (L) and Alexander Goehr with his paternal grandparents, Gertrud and Julius. Goehr Archive | 41 |
| Michael Tippett and Walter Goehr. Goehr Archive | 46 |
| Richard Hall. Courtesy of the Royal Northern College of Music | 53 |
| Olivier Messiaen. Photo by Laelia Goehr | 66 |
| Yvonne Loriod. Photo by Laelia Goehr | 69 |
| Alexander Goehr with Pierre Boulez, late 1950s. Goehr Archive | 82 |
| Hanns Eisler in Hollywood, 1943. Courtesy of Eisler-Haus Leipzig | 108 |
| Alan Hacker. Photo by Laelia Goehr | 120 |
| Arnold Schoenberg, Berlin class, with Walter Goehr over his left shoulder. Goehr Archive | 126 |
| Ulrich Siegele, 2022. Photo by Linda Koldau | 146 |
| Alexander Goehr, 1960s. Photo by Laelia Goehr | 150 |
| Walter Goehr conducting. Goehr Archive | 214 |

**MUSICAL EXAMPLES**

**Example 1.** Pentatonic scale with harmonic derivations　　54

**Example 2.** Twelve-tone row with hexachordal harmonic derivations from *Chaconne for Winds, Op. 34.*　　58

**Example 3a.** Cantus from *Psalm 4, op. 38a*　　173

**Example 3b.** Psalm 4 cantus with "white note" harmony　　174

**Example 3c.** Psalm 4 cantus with "black note" harmony　　174

*Sally Groves and Alexander Goehr. Sally Groves Collection*

**FOREWORD**
*By Sally Groves*

This is a profound, generous, and illuminating book. Sandy has always taken a delight in sharing thoughts, observations, and curiosity with his friends, many of them former students. One never feels put down in such conversations, in which there is always a wonderful sense of exploration. So it is marvelous that Jack has managed to capture the spirit of those conversations and lead us out into such a rich landscape.

Thank you, Sandy. The musical DNA is all there in this book, waiting to be explored.

*Jack Van Zandt and Alexander Goehr. Photo by Julia Crockatt*

**PREFACE**
*By Jack Van Zandt*

In December of 1976, I traveled from my home in warm Southern California to freezing cold Cambridge to begin studies as a private composition student of Alexander "Sandy" Goehr, who had just become the Professor of Music there. Our first meeting in his studio at Trinity Hall is etched in my memory, and I describe this in my Introduction that follows. During 1977, I spent nearly a year as his private pupil, and then returned in 1978 as an official PhD student under him at the university. I became his teaching assistant and then his personal musical assistant, which concluded in April 1985 with the premiere of his opera *Behold the Sun*, for which I had spent many years working on the complete score, parts, and piano reduction. From the early 1980s into the mid-1990s, I lived in Ireland and during that time, we would exchange letters and phone calls, and I would visit him in Cambridge when I could and he visited me in Ireland. I returned to the U.S. in 1996 and we continued to keep in touch, and of course I followed his work and was able to hear some of his performances and premieres whenever I was in the U.K.

In 2010, I flew to the U.K. to stay with Sandy and his wife, Amira, and attend a performance of his then new opera, *Promised End*, in Cambridge. During that visit, we enjoyed a few late nights discussing many things over some very good Irish single malt whiskey. I was especially interested in our conversations about the relationship between teachers and students of composition and how our art form is transferred via that relationship through the generations.

As a result of those chats, Sandy asked me to edit his essay "Learning to Compose," which outlines his journey as a composer, student, and teacher. (I should mention that I had worked as a book editor for several years in the 1990s.)

The process of going through the editorial process with him allowed me the pleasure of remembering the more than four decades he had been my teacher, mentor, and friend, as well as bringing my own journey as a composer into sharper focus. It also gave me the opportunity to consider and appreciate what the gift of those decades has meant to me.

Since that essay was published, we have—thanks to the advent of technology and the invention of Skype—been able to carry on discussing and elaborating on the matters Sandy wrote about in "Learning to Compose," and we have spent a lot of time talking about how someone goes about learning to be a composer, and how we as teachers are best able to guide our pupils from our own experiences. Through those recorded conversations, we developed the idea for a book about musical "DNA" and how it evolves and is passed on from one generation to the next.

To create *Composing a Life: Teachers, Mentors, and Models*, Sandy and I discussed his experiences as a student of individual composers and mentors—his father Walter Goehr, Richard Hall, Michael Tippett, Olivier Messiaen, Yvonne Loriod, Hanns Eisler, Pierre Boulez, Ulrich Siegele, Milton Babbitt, and others. Then we went on to talk about the ways he put those lessons to practical use as a composer to create his unique approach utilizing the compositional subjects discussed in the second part of the book—such as modeling, figured bass, modality, and text setting—and how all of this is reflected in his mentorship of his students. I wanted to understand how he filtered his life and experiences into teaching processes that benefited me as his student, and how I in turn further filtered what I learned from him to create my music and teach my students. Going through the process of creating this book with Sandy has also given me a unique insight into his life and work that has gone beyond what I already knew from my past experiences with him.

Something that we discussed for many years is how the tradition of music in the context of human culture, from the prehistoric past to the present, is like the Ganges in Hindu myth, a continuum, and that the practice of creating music is still handed down across the ages by successive generations of teachers to pupils, who become teachers, etc. This is the case for all music anywhere in human existence, not just Western classical music. However, the transgenerational evolution and passing on of musical DNA is rarely talked about and is not completely understood. We hope this book will change that and will inspire composers and teachers to examine their own musical experiences and heritage in this way.

In practical terms, the text of this book is drawn from recordings of dozens of conversations we had via the Internet between Cambridge and Los Angeles, beginning in 2016 and continuing into 2023. Transcripts of some of these conversations that we chose as fitting the theme of this book were made and edited by me, and then we met in Cambridge or worked remotely to shape the material into the final form presented here.

The book is divided into two main parts with an Interlude between Parts I and II and final Coda. Part I is autobiographical and its focus is on influential experiences as well as on the individuals who were the major teachers and mentors in Goehr's development toward becoming a composer, and who have affected his work right up to the present. We structured the text of the chapters in Part I by my introducing the subject and then getting out of the way so the reader can get an uninterrupted picture of Goehr's learning experiences, with my questions or ideas for elaboration or clarification integrated into the flow of his text.

For the Interlude and the chapters in Part II, we produced an edited version of our conversations to show how they transpired, and to give the reader an idea of our continuing teacher-student relationship. We both felt that these subjects were important to his work and evolution as a composer.

The Interlude, about Goehr's experiences in America, details the time he spent teaching (New England Conservatory and Yale) and traveling in the U.S. in the 1960s and 70s, and the composers who influenced him and became his friends. The young Goehr's time in America mirrors my experiences as an American student and young composer in the U.K., especially since all my composition teachers and mentors were British (Goehr, Peter Fricker, Thea Musgrave, Peter Maxwell Davies, Harrison Birtwistle, and Peter Zinovieff).

The chapter about Goehr's father, Walter—the conductor, the composer, and the pupil of Schoenberg—we decided to save for last, for the Coda. Readers will easily understand the reason for this when they get there. The material for this concluding essay was drawn from several of our conversations which we edited into the present text, with Sandy putting on the finishing touches.

My essay that begins the book proper aims to introduce what follows, as well as to paint a picture of what it was like to be pupil and friend for most of my life and what it's meant to me personally and as a composer and teacher. I hope it serves to offer a deeper understanding of the subject of the transfer of musical DNA from teacher to student and how this relationship can work if the circumstances are right.

*Jack Van Zandt. Photo by Elisa Ferarri*

**ALEXANDER GOEHR
COMPOSING A LIFE**

*Alexander Goehr and Jack Van Zandt, 21 December 1979.*
*Jack Van Zandt Collection*

# INTRODUCTION
Notes From My Apprenticeship: *Zen in the Art of Composing*
By Jack Van Zandt

> *The Japanese pupil brings with him three things: good education, passionate love for his chosen art, and uncritical veneration of his teacher. The teacher-pupil relationship has belonged since ancient times to the basic commitments of life and therefore presupposes, on the part of the teacher, a high responsibility which goes far beyond the scope of his professional duties.*
>
> Eugen Herrigel, *Zen in the Art of Archery*

The greatest teachers are the rare ones who profoundly change you as a human being and whose lessons affect you throughout a lifetime. For me, Alexander "Sandy" Goehr has been that teacher. Since the day I became his pupil in Cambridge in December 1976, he has been the most important influence on my musical and intellectual life as my teacher, mentor, colleague, and close friend.

Conducting our special recorded conversations over the past several years has provided me with an opportunity to consider the intersection between my journey in life and his. As I have gone on to become both composer and teacher—and always a student of our art—I know that learning music or any skill or art requires more than the study of some form of mathematical or set theory analysis. There is an intellectual intimacy between venerated teachers and passionate students, and when they click, the result is a two-way street that affects both. I find this happening with the young musicians I mentor, and, with many of them, that contact means as much to me as it does to them. That is something that I learned from Sandy. If you treat the students who look up to you with the utmost respect, you get the same in return, sometimes tenfold, and your effect as a teacher is very much greater.

So, how did a young music student from Southern California get all the way to Sandy Goehr in Cambridge in 1976?

The American novelist Kurt Vonnegut was once asked by an interviewer to describe his life in one sentence. He thought briefly, and then said: "I was a victim of a series of accidents, as are we all." I have always felt this simple statement to be profound, and find that it describes my life and anyone else's I know just as well.

My own youthful journey from my native California to mid-1970s Cambridge to study with Sandy was itself an accident. Graduating midterm in the final year of my BA degree program at the University of California at Santa Barbara left me with some time to fill before my planned graduate study. I was feeling a little bit at loose ends and approached my teacher at the time, Peter Racine Fricker, a wonderful man, composer, and excellent teacher himself, for advice as to what I should do in the meantime. Fricker, noticing that I was carrying around a few scores of Goehr's music (the *Little Symphony*, *Pastorals* for orchestra, the Second String Quartet, and the Piano Trio), asked what I thought of them. I said that I liked them very much and that I thought they were "original, unusual, and idiosyncratic." Fricker said that he was an old friend of Goehr's and suggested that I go to England and study privately with him, which I found incredibly exciting. To cut a long story short, parents were consulted, letters were exchanged (my other teacher at the time, Thea Musgrave, who had inspired my investigations into contemporary British music that led me to discover Goehr, also sent a letter of recommendation to Sandy), my student scores were airmailed to Sandy in Leeds at his request, and I soon found myself in cold, frozen Cambridge in December of 1976, the first year of Sandy's long reign there as Professor of Music.

It seemed at first as if it might have been a case of oil and water. Sandy, the highly intelligent, extremely well-read teacher and composer with the European pedigree steeped in tradition, and me, the California hippie with my ordinary but good educational career, and musical background of alto saxophonist in school bands and rock guitarist. I was a Johnny-come-lately to serious music composition due to a chance encounter with Schoenberg's Violin Concerto at the age of eighteen. What I know now that I didn't know then was that Sandy, like me, had come to music composition relatively late in a way that mirrored my own short journey at that time. Like Sandy in his youth, I had found ways to compensate for what I lacked to get to where I wanted to go. What I didn't know filled a much bigger bag than what I did know, but I was determined to figure it all out and do it in my own way. I think because Sandy had essentially done it in a similar fashion, he understood what I was up to much more than I did myself, and he was uniquely prepared and able to help me. Many a lesser teacher at Sandy's level of expertise surely would have sent me home to California to sharpen my skills or give up!

I still vividly remember that first lesson in his rooms at Trinity Hall in early January 1977, and how nervous I was. I immediately got down to business inquiring as to how much I would be paying for the lessons. He asked, "Are you a rich man or a poor man?" "Well, definitely not rich," I said. "I usually get fifteen pounds for a weekly lesson," he ventured. I gulped; I came from a working class family, and although we weren't poor, money was tight. "That will be fine," I said, "but I will only be able to afford to come every other week." Without missing a beat, Sandy smiled and said, "Don't worry; how about we say eight pounds a week then." That was a huge relief to me as I had around 1,500 pounds to live on for the entire year. (After three months or so, Sandy stopped taking payment from me saying I had paid enough!)

I then naively asked what he had thought of the scores that I had sent to him. He replied (in a very cordial manner), "Well, you could be better than you are, but if you were, you probably wouldn't need me." It wasn't the last stupid question I asked in my life, but it was, however, a very good lesson in humility for the pampered kid far away from home and doting parents for the first time.

In retrospect, at twenty-two I was a pretty green young composer, but eager and willing to learn how to get better. Thanks to Sandy's guidance, I managed to learn and improve, and I am still doing it. Looking back over five decades, with the advantage of knowing what I have learned in the meantime and with the experience of being a teacher myself, I have a very personal perspective on Sandy the teacher; and, of course, I have the extra added benefit of having discussed the experience with many other Goehr pupils over the years. It should be remembered that Sandy has taught many hundreds of composers from all over the world in his life, and he is certainly one of the most important composition teachers of the past sixty years or so. Some of my fellow Goehr pupils are Anthony Gilbert, David Ward, Edward Cowie, George Benjamin, Geoff Poole, Julian Anderson, Thomas Adès, Robin Holloway, Silvina Milstein, Nicholas Cook, Bayan Northcott, Nicholas Sackman, Roger Smalley, and Emma-Ruth Richards; Australians Ann Carr-Boyd and Colin Burnby; Israeli Michael Wolpe, and Americans Zhou Long, Chen Yi, David Froom, Daria Semegen, Harold Meltzer, David Babcock, and Joan Huang.

Going back to Vonnegut, if you are a student of Goehr's, you know that the concept of an "accident" is seminal to his teaching method and a distinctive feature of his compositional process. One of the first things he taught me was to embrace the "happy accident" and make something of it; even make your whole piece about it, or several more pieces if it is justified. It is often the accident and resulting unforeseen consequences that will propel pieces above and beyond the mechanics of their creation, transcending the preoccupation with "getting from one note to the next" as Sandy puts it, and becoming something original.

One of the unique qualities that make Sandy an excellent teacher is that he is able to abstract practical methods from his own experiences and struggles as a composer to help those who are going through similar struggles of their own. He believes that failure is a necessary learning experience and an opportunity to improve. His great strength comes from recognizing exactly what an individual student composer is having difficulties with, then giving them the intellectual tools to surmount those problems, and guiding them to finding their way. He never, ever, imposes his own way of working as a composer on a student as a solution. He nearly always sees and understands the way each of his students is working. By putting himself in their place, he can make them see things according to their own methods.

One of Sandy's early suggestions to me was to always set a specific task for myself as the first step to writing a new piece. At the time, I was coming up with schemes and structural inventions for organizing music without having a clue as to how I would use them. He made me think about what sort of sound I wanted to create first and to come up with an ensemble for which I could complete such a sonic design. Once I set my sights on a specific group of instruments and the particular sound I wanted, then, he said, I could let my propensity to create structural coherence loose on making *that* noise with *those* instruments. It was a new way of thinking for me then (even though it now seems obvious as the way I should work) that has served me well ever since.

I can give some examples that I remember from my own early period of study with Sandy. I had been studying the string quartets of Bartók and was experimenting with adapting some of his structural techniques on a wider scale in a new piece, but was having trouble making it yield anything that went on for very long before fizzling out. Sandy led me through several examples from Bartók and we sketched out some possible ways of proceeding using the material I had invented for my piece. Within an hour I had worked out a methodology with Sandy's guidance and the piece became my Opus One, a string trio. That lesson became one of my tools and is still relevant to my work today.

I was (and still am today) fascinated with canonic writing and was attempting all sorts of different combinations in a post-tonal language, which weren't entirely successful. Sandy advised me to study the Five Canons, op. 16, of Webern, and he explained to me in minute detail how Webern created them in such a way that I was able to begin to do it myself after several practice runs. He suggested that I try and write a set of canonic studies for two like instruments, and I composed such a set for two violins. Following on with this study, Sandy also suggested we study Gregorian chant and explained how chants were employed as a *cantus firmus* by mediaeval and Renaissance composers in creating elaborate polyphonic compositions around the existing material. Of course I was familiar with this period of early music from concerts and recordings, as well as my studies in music history and theory, but this was the first time I actually considered *how* they were composed. Thus began a lifelong love and study of early choral music that has also been hugely influential in my own way of composing.

Another of his lessons that was important to me that I have passed on to my students was his method to get over a serious block and back to composing. (I am not sure what source he adapted it from, but it may have been *Zen in the Art of Archery*.) It has worked for me even in the worst of times when I thought I would never be able to compose again.

Sandy told me, first of all, to create a ritual to follow each and every day that leads up to composing. At that time for me it was to lay out my manuscript paper, sharpen a stack of pencils, have my erasers, straight edges, etc., all lined up nearby and everything ready to go. Then, you take up a newly sharpened pencil and you start writing whatever notes come to you in whatever fashion on the manuscript, improvising onto paper stream-of-consciousness style, and keep going no matter what. At any point if the notes you are writing come together structurally and start to make some sort of sense to you, immediately crumple up the paper and throw it away. Then, take up a new sharp pencil and a fresh sheet of paper and do the same thing again. After half a dozen attempts or so, you will find that your facility has returned and that you can continue with whatever piece it is that you are working on. I have thought about how it is that this method usually works, and I think it is because, under pressure, your unconscious mind takes over and starts to involve and permutate processes that you have already been employing in your work, and suddenly a solution jumps out and appears on the paper (or, these days, on the computer screen). At least, that's the way it seems to go for me.

I have never found a composer that Sandy did not have a personal perspective on, whether he had an artistic interest in them or not. When I was first studying with him my favored earlier composers were Schoenberg (first and foremost), Ives, Stravinsky, Webern, Varèse, Debussy, Ravel, and Scriabin, and the recent and living composers I most admired (other than Goehr) were Dallapiccola, Carter, Ligeti, Messiaen, Boulez, Berio, Nono, Krenek, and Xenakis. He discussed all these composers with me in some detail, helping me to develop my critical facilities and analytical skills in order to apply what I learned from them to my own way of thinking and composing. At the time, Sandy was very interested in figured bass and he helped me appreciate a group of composers that I was only vaguely familiar with at the time: Scarlatti, Rameau, C.P.E. Bach, Couperin, and, more than anyone else, Handel. We also delved into the early English choral composers (in the wake of our studies of chant), and I have a special love for this music—from Dunstable to Byrd—to this day because of those lessons.

Another important aspect of this period of my study with Sandy was reading the ongoing list of his book suggestions and the subsequent discussions we had about them. Lucky for me that I was a voracious reader because it was all I could do to keep up with his "suggestions." Something that seemed odd to me at the time but I later came to understand is that I was not encouraged to read any analytical or theoretical books on contemporary music. When I asked about this, Sandy said I should learn to compose by listening and doing and that no after-the-fact theory of music was going to help me do either. What I did do, according to his prompting, was read books on art, aesthetics, ethnomusicology, history, philosophy, theater and cinema, literature, and poetry. He also had me reading across the board geographically—American (Sandy has a great appreciation for and knowledge of American culture), European, and Asian—something that was rare at the time. What he was getting me to do was to understand what we were doing as composers in the context of world culture and helping me find ways to reflect these discoveries back into my own musical work. This set up a crucially important habitual pattern in me that is still a very big part of my daily activity.

For example, I remember early on we started discussing Paul Klee's *Pedagogical Sketchbook*, followed by his notebooks *The Nature of Nature* and *The Thinking Eye*. At one lesson we discussed Klee's concept of "taking a line for a walk" and how it could be applied to composing. We discussed many artists at the time that seemed particularly appropriate to musicians, including Picasso, Jackson Pollock, Henry Moore, the Italian and Russian futurists, and Kandinsky, especially his *Concerning the Spiritual in Art* and the *Blaue Reiter* writings.

After attending a performance of Sandy's *Sonata about Jerusalem* in London, I expressed an interest in composing political music theater and was sent off to read Erwin Piscator's *Political Theatre*, Eisenstein's collected writings on the theory of cinema, and a book on Noh and Kabuki whose title I have forgotten, all works that had been important to Sandy's development of his music theater triptych (*Naboth's Vineyard, Sonata about Jerusalem,* and *Shadowplay*) and numerous other theatrical works and operas (including *Arden Must Die, Behold the Sun, Arianna,* and *Promised End*). We have had many discussions over the years on this subject and it made me an avid student of film and theater theory, which I still am today.

In my undergraduate years in Santa Barbara, I had been a devotee of the works of Orwell, Huxley, Hesse, the aforementioned Vonnegut, and a long list of science fiction authors. Sandy got me reading Joyce and Beckett (two authors that would assume a special significance for me later when I took up citizenship and residence in Ireland), and Kafka and Mann. I also began to become familiar with the linguistic works of Noam Chomsky at this time, as well as the philosophical works of Wittgenstein and others. Our discussions stimulated my great interest in the parallels and differences between music and language as well as the origins and history of the development of both.

More directly to the point of my musical studies, I was reading a lot of poetry at the time and we often discussed poetry and music and their close relationship. I was setting some poems by the surrealist Rafael Alberti in the original Spanish to music, for soprano and chamber orchestra, and Sandy guided me through discovering the best way of doing so. I was "noodling about" too much in his opinion, and so we started by my reading the poems out loud, and then writing down the words with the rhythm I used while reading. The result was a revelation to me. I was trying too hard to cover far too much territory with the words in a way that was not intended by the poet. Sandy taught me to respect the nature of the original and preserve the integrity of the poet's creation by "reading" it into my musical setting.

After several months, Sandy suggested that I should get "a different perspective from another composer" while I was visiting England. He arranged for me to attend Peter Maxwell "Max" Davies's class at the Dartington Summer School that year (1977). Everyone knows that once upon a time in the 1950s, Sandy, Max, and Harry Birtwistle were the primary members of what was called the "Manchester School" of composers, and for a period of time they were all very close friends and colleagues, along with the pianist John Ogdon and trumpeter/conductor Elgar Howarth. By 1977, however, that was all in the past. Sandy and Max had taken separate paths and their friendship was no longer as close as it had once been (though they became closer again in Max's later years). Considering the situation, it was all the more amazing to me that Sandy would write to Max on my behalf and that Max would take me in the class that was restricted to eight students, of which I was the last admitted. (I was already very much a fan of Max's music—especially *Eight Songs for a Mad King* and the Second Taverner *Fantasia*—and of his ensemble, The Fires of London.)

Apart from being a big boost to my self-confidence, attending Max's intense and very long daily classes was an eye-opening experience for me and a perfect place for me to get "perspective" on my time with Sandy so far. I learned a hell of a lot, and applying what I had learned from Sandy to the work we were required to do at Dartington paid dividends with Max, who knew very well where I had picked the stuff up. In retrospect, I would say that Max was very careful with me and I think he paid close attention to me, making sure I got something out of the summer that I could take back to Cambridge. It was a wonderful experience, one of the most important in my life, and I met a lot of new people and made many friends there. But the important thing to remember in this context is that I only went to Max in the first place because it was part of Sandy's plan for me as his student to get the most out of my time in England. He wanted me to go home to California having learned a great deal and having had some life-changing experiences. (I think it was also a signal of professional and personal respect for Max and vice versa.)

After my first ten-month period in Cambridge, I returned to California only briefly—long enough to make some money and apply through official channels to become a foreign PhD student at Cambridge under Goehr. I had found my place for the next stage of life quite by accident.

I returned in late 1978 to Cambridge and to Sandy as an official grad student, though from day one, my unofficial position was something altogether different. I was almost immediately conscripted (most willingly) by him into service as a teaching, music and personal assistant. Thus began what I call my "apprenticeship" in an old-fashioned sense, something that is rare in this day and age.

So, what was this apprenticeship exactly? I began to fill the role of teaching assistant, helping to plan and organize a few undergraduate courses, a weekly student composer seminar and events with visiting lecturers, composers, and players. I remember one course that was a music perception lab where we played Webern's *Symphony*, Boulez's *Structures* and Debussy's *Prélude à l'après-midi d'un faune*, among other pieces, and the students would discuss and analyze the music only from what they heard, not from any printed score.

My fellow PhD student, music theorist Nicholas Cook, was also involved in running this course.

At the weekly composer meeting, undergraduate students would come to Sandy's Trinity Hall rooms, play their pieces and discuss them, or some other topic chosen by Sandy. Mostly the pieces would be what you would expect from student composers anywhere in the world, but one student clearly stood out from the rest. George Benjamin had come to Cambridge to study with Sandy after a time in Paris with Messiaen. Even then, as a teenager, his music was already at a very high level sonically, as you would expect from a Messiaen pupil, but he needed the kind of structured thinking that Sandy is so good at teaching to give his pieces some depth.

These were very important learning experiences for me in terms of becoming a teacher in the future, but other duties were more important to my growth as a composer. I was drafted in as a musical assistant to Sandy the composer, a role that took on increasing significance over the coming years. At this time, in early 1979, Sandy was composing *Babylon the Great Is Fallen*, four large-scale pieces for chorus and orchestra, to fulfill a commission from the BBC Symphony and Chorus. These pieces would become the musical/dramatic pillars on which he would hang his next opera, *Behold the Sun*. My first job was to prepare the orchestral score (as it progressed from week to week) and, later, the parts for the performance. It was fascinating for me to get an inside look on how Sandy worked from sketches to a short score, giving me the indications for the final orchestral score, followed by a series of revisions.

I moved into his house during the summer of 1979, to facilitate the work on *Babylon the Great Is Fallen* (which was premiered by the BBC Symphony under Michael Gielen at the Royal Festival Hall on December 12, 1979). Sandy took a sabbatical around this time and went on an extended trip to China that was financed by the British Council, becoming the first Western composer to make an official visit there in many years. I remember helping him prepare some lectures for the visit. There were trips to Europe and Israel during this time, and it was during an extended residence in Jerusalem that he met his wife, the Israeli sinologist Amira Katz.

Back in his home, Sandy composed several new pieces while I was living in his house. After *Babylon the Great Is Fallen* there were other sections of the upcoming opera, including the stunningly beautiful aria *Behold the Sun*, op. 44a, which was one of the first times Sandy's experiments with figured bass and adaptations of quasi-tonal harmony yielded the fresh, original sound world that his works have inhabited ever since. Also during my time there, he composed *Sinfonia*, *op. 42*, *Deux Etudes, op. 43* for orchestra, and the Kafka songs for voice and piano, *Das Gesetz der Quadrille, op. 41*. I attended the premieres of all these works.

I was amazed at how Sandy could fulfill the enormous responsibilities of being the Cambridge Professor of Music and at the same time compose one work after another without much space for rest in between. He used to get up very early in the morning and I would hear him in his study playing bits over and over on the piano with slight variations while singing/humming in an "unearthly" harmony. This would begin at 5 a.m. most mornings and continue until breakfast, after which he would be off to the day job during term weekdays, leaving me behind most days to get on with the work in his studio.

I was lucky enough to watch and hear these works come into being from conception to the premiere performances. I learned much by observing and asking questions about how Sandy was working. He would show me his sketches and how they progressed. I understood his idiosyncratic "modal serialism" system of composing that he had developed from Schoenberg's twelve-tone technique, but since he had undergone a kind of compositional overhaul in 1976 with his three *Psalm 4* works—which led him in a completely new direction—he was composing music so different from mine or anyone else's that I was mystified and intrigued by it at the same time. It gave me a new appreciation of music traditions and history and also made me realize that music did not have to be ultra-complicated and anti-tonal to be something revolutionary, fresh and new.

Another part of my continuing education took place around the kitchen dining table. Much of this was one on one: we talked about books we'd read, music we'd heard, art exhibitions and films we'd seen, etc. Sandy would often challenge a statement or interpretation I made and urge me to explain or defend it. These conversations really developed my critical skills and I learned to think before I spoke up and ventured an opinion.

Also at that dining table was a succession of dinner parties. Some of the many guests who regularly gathered around that table over the years and whom I came to know included composers Harry Birtwistle, Hugh Wood, and Robin Holloway; composer/conductor Ryan Wigglesworth; the head of new music at Schott and Co., Sally Groves; Cambridge philosopher Bernard Williams; Nobel Prize-winning economist Sir James Mirrlees; electronic and computer music pioneer Peter Zinovieff; Boosey and Hawkes managing director David Drew and his wife, Judy; BBC executive Jimmy Burnett and his wife, Janet; Cambridge music lecturer Iain Fenlon; and ethnomusicologist Simha Arom and his wife, Sonia. Many of those conversations have stuck with me and I often think of how much I learned from them about music, art, philosophy, literature, and other things.

I attended countless concerts and premieres with Sandy over the years and was introduced by him to many interesting people before and after them. I remember meeting a young (thirty-seven) Maurizio Pollini after the premiere of *Babylon the Great Is Fallen* at the Royal Festival Hall. Pollini had played in the performance of Beethoven's choral fantasy in the same concert. I also received introductions to composers and conductors—including Oliver Knussen, Pierre Boulez, David Atherton, and Michael Gielen—and many leading performers. My head spins when I think of it now, but in retrospect it seems it was all part of my education. I learned that well-known figures are just people like everybody else, and you can talk to them as easily as someone in your own family (sometimes more easily!). Because of those experiences, I developed the ability to talk to anyone about anything at any time without feeling nervous, something that has served me well throughout my life.

Even after I left Cambridge and moved to London and then Ireland, I continued to assist Sandy until 1985. I spent more than two years (1982–5) preparing the orchestral score and parts for the premiere performance of his massive three-act opera *Behold the Sun, op. 44*, in Germany in April 1985. I thought I knew quite a bit about orchestration, but working on that huge project was like going to orchestration graduate school. As Sandy finished portions of the score, we would get together in his studio and spend a couple of days going over the orchestral design. We would make rough sketches for me to work from. Sometimes Sandy would give me a list of instruments and let me decide the exact deployment of the orchestration for a short section, which was much appreciated and very encouraging. I would complete a full pencil draft on manuscript paper at my cottage in Ireland, and then return to Cambridge to show it to Sandy who would make the final changes and adjustments (sometimes they were extensive). Then I would return to Ireland to make the final copy on vellum in ink. This would get looked at one more time by Sandy and then I would make any last corrections in Cambridge before taking them to the production office at Schott and Co. on

Great Marlborough Street in London on my way back home to Ireland.

The premiere of *Behold the Sun* by Deutsche Oper am Rhein in Duisburg, Germany, on April 19, 1985, which I attended, marked the end of my nearly nine years as Sandy's pupil and assistant. By then, I had moved to Ireland and had become a music teacher myself. All of my students have benefited from the teaching methods I learned from Sandy, and a few of them have gone on to become professional music teachers, performers, and composers and are continuing the "tradition." It always cheers me up to think about this fact. It is an honor to pass on Sandy's teachings to the next generations and to know that they will continue long after our time on planet Earth.

My position as Sandy's pupil did not end in 1985, and it never will. Over the years it has continued, albeit at a slightly different pace and level of discussion, given that I now live in Los Angeles. Thanks to modern technology, we are in fairly regular contact through the magic of the Internet, and I go to Cambridge for a visit of a few days whenever I can.

I thought about making a list of items that I learned from Sandy over the years, but I realized that would be impossible, because, in a sense, everything I have learned since the first day we met in 1976 has been influenced by him in some way. There hasn't been a day that has gone by in the years since that I have not used something I learned from Sandy in my life, either as composer, teacher, and writer, as I am today, or as a book editor and publisher, as I made my living in the 1990s. The development of project management skills and powers of self-initiative that I learned working with Sandy have proven crucial for what I have accomplished in life so far. Reflecting back over the years to try and put it in a nutshell, I see that the great lesson I learned from him is that it isn't the destination in life that is important but the journey: Music *is* life, and life *is* music. My gratitude to him for this and everything else I learned from him, and the delight and joy of our many years of friendship, knows no bounds.

> *Steep is the way to mastery. Often nothing keeps the pupil on the move but his faith in his teacher, whose mastery is now beginning to dawn on him. He is a living example of the inner work, and he convinces by his mere presence.*
>
> *How far the pupil will go is not the concern of the teacher and Master. Hardly has he shown him the right way when he must let him go on alone. There is only one thing more he can do to help him endure the loneliness: he turns him away from himself, from the Master, by exhorting him to go further than he himself has done, and to "climb on the shoulders of his teacher."*
>
> *Wherever his way may take him, the pupil, though he may lose sight of his teacher, can never forget him. With a gratitude as great as the uncritical veneration of the beginner, as strong as the saving faith of the artist, he can now take his Master's place, ready for any sacrifice. Countless examples down to the recent past testify that this gratitude far exceeds the measure of what is customary among mankind.*
>
> *Eugen Herrigel, Zen in the Art of Archery*

# PART I:
# TEACHERS AND MENTORS

*Alexander Goehr as a young man, 1940s.
Photo by Laelia Goehr*

## 1. BEGINNINGS

*JVZ: Goehr rarely talks about details of his early life or his family history, but in answer to my request that he do so for this book, to give important background context to his music student years and beyond, he graciously agreed to go into the subject on the record. Over the decades he has told me many stories and anecdotes from his youth which I have found fascinating, and so I was able to ask him specific questions that guided him through some of those stories in our discussion dedicated to his childhood and family memories.*

*Born in 1932 in Berlin, he has no memory of the city as his parents left Germany and brought him to England when he was an infant. His father, Walter Goehr (1903–60), a native Berliner and pupil of Schoenberg's in the 1920s, was a well-known conductor and composer who worked for the BBC before and during the Second World War and through the 1950s. His photographer mother Laelia (née Rivlin, 1908–2002) had studied piano in her native Kyiv, which was then in Russia. After the Russian Revolution she moved to Berlin, where she later worked as a professional musician and met Walter. So music was in Goehr's blood and in his life from the very beginning.*

*I began our conversation by asking him about his earliest memories of his family home in Buckinghamshire, including his witnessing the bombing of distant London during the Blitz. He continued by talking about his school days, his parents, and the war work that they did.*

AG: Many of my earliest memories come from our home in Amersham, Buckinghamshire, where my parents had bought a house for us to move into from London in 1940 in order to escape the German bombing. We lived in comparative comfort outside London, and my father went into work every day by train to the BBC where he was involved in creating war propaganda. There was a shelter in the garden that was high up on a hill looking out towards distant London, and I was able to see the searchlights at night catching the Luftwaffe bombers during the Battle of Britain. Luckily we were far enough away not to have bombs falling nearby. I remember my father listening to Hitler's speeches on the radio and laughing at them, although they weren't funny.

One day in 1940, I went with my mother to a matinee showing at the local cinema of *The Bad Man of Wyoming*. Coming out in the fading evening light, the sky was black with German planes. The Luftwaffe would come across the Channel in the late afternoon to bomb targets at night, and this particular evening they were probably on their way to attack one of the northern industrial cities. It might have been Coventry, but I am not sure. We couldn't hear them as they were much too high, but they covered the entire sky.

My mother, Laelia Rivlin, born in 1908, was from Kyiv, which was then in Russia. She studied piano at the Kyiv Conservatory and lived next door to Vladimir Horowitz. Her first public performance, of *Butterflies* by Grieg, was in the same concert that Horowitz was doing his final recital. My maternal grandfather, being bourgeois, left Russia quite early after the Revolution, in 1919 or so, and went to Germany. My mother and her two brothers, along with their mother, stayed on in Kyiv until about 1921, when they escaped to Poland and then on to Berlin where my grandfather was trying to earn a living of some sort. Neither of my grandparents was musical, so my mother was the first musician in her family.

My father, Walter, was born in Berlin in 1903. His mother, Thekla, was musical. Her maiden name was Mendelssohn, but she was not a relative of the composer. I didn't know her, as she died before I was born. My grandfather Julius Goehr owned a textile factory in Berlin until the Nazis confiscated it. He lived in hiding in Berlin during the Second World War.

*Walter Goehr (L) and Alexander Goehr with his paternal grandparents, Gertrud and Julius. Goehr Archive*

He had married a Christian, Gertrud, after the death of my grandmother, and so was not deported to the camps like other Jews. He stayed in Berlin after the war and came to England for visits, so I remember him. He died in 1947, the same year I took my school certificate.

My father and his younger brother, Rudolph ("Rudy"), were musicians from an early age. My father played the piano and my Uncle Rudy played the violin. My father started conducting operettas when he was about eighteen, and was successful from an early age at getting such jobs. Both brothers had conventional music studies with various teachers, and then went to the *Hochschule* and studied with Schoenberg in his Berlin class around 1927–8.

One of my father's friends in the class was Winfried Zillig, a huge Bavarian who was the wartime director of the Kraków Opera. He delivered food parcels during the war to my grandfather Julius Goehr when he was in hiding in Berlin, and I met him in the 1950s. Roberto Gerhard was also in the class, as was the Greek Nikos Skalkottas, who was my father's best friend in the class and who became a very prominent composer. My father said that Schoenberg thought the most gifted student in the class was Norbert von Hannenheim, about whom very little is known except that he died just after the war. It was long believed that all his scores were destroyed, but several of his works have since been found.

All these composers in the class at the time composed music that was like Schoenberg's *Suite for Piano, op. 25*, but with gentler harmony. However, my father didn't stay a strict Schoenbergian after his studies. He became good friends with Kurt Weill and Hanns Eisler, worked in the theater as a conductor, and became the music director in the company of the epic theater director Erwin Piscator. My father moved in the Weill and Hindemith world of actors and musicians, rather than the Schoenberg world, though his pieces of that time show someone who has been trained by Schoenberg trying to compose pieces like Weill.

My father composed for the theater and cinema, as well as producing concert music, and even had a symphony performed at this time. He also worked for Berlin Radio, writing incidental music for radio plays and adaptations of novels. German radio was very advanced then and model radio programs were created there that influenced productions all over Europe, including the BBC. He was conducting the music sessions for many of these radio and theater productions, but it was only after we came to England subsequent to my birth in 1932 that he became a concert conductor.

My mother and her best friend, Rosa Goldstein, had a piano duo act called the Stone Sisters. They took the stage names of Lil and Peggy Stone, as English names were very fashionable then. They were quite well known and played light popular German music, jazz, swing, and ragtime music in cabarets, restaurants, clubs, and bars in various European countries.

My parents met in 1929 or 1930 at a party in Billy Wilder's house in Berlin. They were introduced at the party by the Polish composer Bronislaw Kaper, who a few years later immigrated to Hollywood, became a very successful film composer, and won an Academy Award in 1954. I was very moved to meet him on one of my trips to California in the 1960s.

My parents and I had the good fortune to come to England just as the Nazis were taking power in Germany. My father was headhunted by the Gramophone Company, the predecessor of EMI, who wanted to find an all-purpose music director who did everything. The company was quite a small outfit then, but my father took the job and we came to England in December of 1932 when I was four months old. It was a very good job and my father made a lot of records, old 78 rpm discs, of course. They were mainly standard classics with some of the best performers and singers of the time, but there were a few modern works as well. Some of the recordings were very successful, and a few still exist.

While my father was making records for the Gramophone Company in the 1930s, he formed a chamber orchestra called the Orchestra Raymonde, which performed mostly light classics arranged by my father once a week. The Raymonde had some of the greatest players of the time in it, like Reg Kell and Arthur Cleghorn, who later emigrated to Hollywood. What made this noteworthy is that at that time, British composers only wrote for large orchestra and string orchestra, and my father, by forming the Raymonde, introduced the Hindemith/Stravinsky/Schoenberg chamber ensemble to England. That was quite an important development because it was completely new at the time in Britain. On the strength of that, my father got a good job at the BBC doing music for war propaganda programs, as he had the ability to orchestrate for smaller ensembles. Today we take this idea of a chamber orchestra for granted, but it didn't exist in England until my father introduced it, and it only became common after the war.

My father arranged music for the propaganda programs twice a week, which were broadcast live, of course. He first did them in London, but was later evacuated to the BBC studios in Manchester. He worked on two programs then. One of his great inspirations and friends was Laurence Gilliam, who was head of BBC Features and Propaganda. They had a program that took place on Wednesdays called "Marching On," which took news stories and sometimes recordings brought to London from the correspondents in the field, and dramatized them with sound effects and music that my father produced, composed, and arranged. They also did a weekly program that was beamed into occupied Europe called "The Shadow of the Swastika."

I was often at the broadcast of these programs with my father when I was home from school for holidays. There were no babysitters, so I went to London with him and some of my earliest musical memories are sitting in those broadcast studios. Because everything was live then, they had sets of studios at the BBC connected by windows. One was music, one was sound effects, another was actors, and it was all like making a film on the spot. It was a complicated undertaking and the programs had to be created and rehearsed within twenty-four hours right up to the live broadcast. My father, who conducted each performance, had several other composers working for him because it was impossible to do all that work himself. His composers were mainly émigrés, like Franz Reizenstein and Mátyás Seiber, because all the English composers were soldiers or otherwise occupied in war duties.

I attended preparatory school in Amersham. At the age of ten I was sent as a boarder to a public school, King Edward VI School in Berkhamsted, largely because my father was doing his BBC work in London and my mother was busy doing her war work, which was photography. She had given up piano playing except at home when she got married. At the beginning of the war, she was working in a camouflage factory, but she didn't much enjoy it. She began to develop skills as a photographer by taking photos of families of the troops to be sent to the soldiers in the field so they would have a picture of their wife and children. Later, she studied in London with Bill Brandt, and worked for the *Picture Post*, which was the most prominent photo journal during and after the war, and a photo magazine called *Lilliput*. She also worked for the *Observer* newspaper and the Hulton Press. After the war my mother became a very busy professional photographer with a home dark room. Lots of her photos later appeared in books, and a volume of her pictures of Stravinsky and other musicians was published in 1987.

I wasn't the best and I wasn't the worst student in my class at Berkhamsted. I was given a relatively good education, one that stayed with me for life and helped form whatever I am to this day. The first two important influences of my life, leaving aside my father, were the composer Michael Tippett, who was in our house a great deal in Amersham, and my Greek and Latin teacher in Berkhamsted, Mr. Hill, an older man who had

*Michael Tippett and Walter Goehr.*
*Goehr Archive*

come back from retirement, as the younger teachers were all away in the military or doing war work. At the time, a student was required to specialize in a subject. I had no scientific interests then, but I liked mathematics. However, I opted for Greek, Latin, and ancient history. By the age of seventeen, I had reached a reasonably high standard in both classical languages. We learned to translate them into English, and to translate English into Greek or Latin, which is more difficult. The texts we translated were usually short passages of classical prose.

I have a memory of one important lesson I received from Mr. Hill. In my translations, my teacher made me realize that even though they weren't bad, they were somewhat superficial. I was imitating the external style, but not getting at the real meaning of the passages I was working on. That memory has stayed with me all my life. I always consider that what I do is slightly superficial at first, and that I have to work hard to get at the real meaning of something. I was affected the same way later when I learned counterpoint from Yvonne Loriod in Paris, and it still is the case with me today, in that I think the first sketches of what I compose tend to be a bit superficial and they need to be worked on to get at what is implicit in the notes. So Mr. Hill was very important for giving me that lesson, and also for helping me develop a love of classical literature that has stayed with me ever since.

There are important moments in school when you find out—whether from a teacher or another student who is doing it better—that you are failing at something or aren't doing it as well as you could, and you suddenly become aware of something that helps you improve. That is when you really learn a lesson that lasts. When I talk about my teachers or someone who has influenced me, I am talking about a very short period of time. In fact, what I got from my teachers might have taken only five minutes! And certainly the period of time when a student and teacher connect is very brief, something like two or three months. I think one of the faults of modern education is that it goes on for too long. The years-long study for PhDs in composition is an embarrassment of sorts. What I learned from my teachers in music took about three months. After that it was a situation of having a friendly coffee or drink with them and being encouraged, but it wasn't the same as those initial short periods. It takes only a split second to really get something. Then you just need to go off and do it!

In our home there was a lot of music, of course, with my mother and father both being musicians. My first musical memories are of trying to compose something at about age six with a few notes on paper, but it didn't make any sense. My mother kept some of my earliest composing efforts consisting of a few minims, some of them on the five lines and some of them not. The first piece I remember trying to play was Stravinsky's *Les Cinq Doigts* (*The Five Fingers*), which is a set of children's pieces.

I had piano, violin, and clarinet lessons as a young boy at home, and sadly I was not very good at any of them! More than learning to play an instrument, I was secretly interested in composition. Because Michael Tippett worked with my father, he came to our house in Amersham a lot, as my father was helping him with the orchestration of his opera *A Midsummer Marriage*, and other things. Tippett was the first person to encourage me, which my father didn't do. I had kept my composing secret until about the age of sixteen or seventeen, and didn't talk about it. I was trying to set poems in Greek and Latin by Horace and Catullus, and also "Preludes" by T.S. Eliot, who was a close friend of Tippett's. (He inspired in me a love of two poets, Eliot and Yeats). Tippett's music of that time was my first experience of modern music and I have had a great love and enthusiasm for his work to this day.

When I finally did tell my father that I was interested in composition, he thought it was ridiculous because I was reasonably good at whatever else I did, but I was not particularly good at that! He was rather hostile to my musical interests, but Tippett spoke up for me and said that I should do whatever I wanted to do and felt deeply about, and whether I was good at it or bad at it was of quite secondary importance. When I finally did take it up, both my father and Tippett, and later my teacher at Manchester, Richard Hall, said, "You take it up for its own sake because you'll never make a penny from it." My father liked to say that Schoenberg didn't make any money from the great pieces he wrote. Later on in my life I did much better than I would have thought then, but I was prepared in my late teens and early twenties to do it for its own sake, and seventy years later I still am: sometimes they pay me and sometimes they don't.

I enjoyed doing lots of things other than music as a boy. For instance I was interested in maps. Under the influence of

Robert Louis Stevenson's *Treasure Island*, I made imaginary maps. These were quite complicated drawings, usually of an island or of towns. In the novel, people found their way to buried treasure using a map, and I became interested in creating maps that would have something that was buried. This aspect of my mapmaking is one of the origins of my compositional practice.

The other great interest of my early teens (which remains to this day) was my fascination with numbers. I was keen on playing cricket and football, and liked to keep track of the statistics from them. An imaginary cricket game I invented, played by throwing dice to score runs, resulted in a whole system of numbers. I still love numbers and I count and calculate everything, such as the number of bars in pieces.

During the war, my boyhood school friends and I were often engaged in fighting the evacuees from London who were rough and tough and who would taunt us and try to beat us up. The food was terrible during the war, so we were always on the hunt for something good and made illicit visits to cafés to eat delicacies—like baked beans on toast or poached eggs—that we could buy with the few pennies of pocket money we had. We would also sneak into the cinema to see a movie if we could. It was really just what normal boys did at that time. Of course, much of our time was spent looking at girls!

Teenagers didn't work then like they do now. I got pocket money from my parents—a small amount, maybe a shilling or a sixpence a week, which doesn't sound like much now, but then it would buy you pencils, ice cream, etc. One of the peculiarities of my father was that I was not allowed to save the pocket money. He insisted that I spend it each week, and if I didn't spend it, he would deduct it from the following week's allowance. Pocket money was to be spent, it wasn't to be saved!

I also had a teacher called Henry Geehl who my father sent me to when I was about seventeen, in 1949. He was an elderly man who lived nearby, a distinguished pianist, composer, and arranger, and a music editor at Edwin Ashdown and Enoch

Publishing Company. It was my first formal musical training, and I studied harmony, counterpoint, and piano with him for about a year. He always wanted me to write the ending cadence for my exercises first, then go to the beginning. I could usually see how to begin and write a cadence at the end, but I had no idea what to do in the middle. I couldn't figure out what chords to use, and I don't think he thought much of me. I did learn to play some Haydn, Mozart, and Beethoven, and up to simpler Schumann. As bad as I was as a pianist, I did manage to work through the scores of Wagner's *Ring* and other big pieces, but I doubt I was very good at it.

At age eighteen in 1950, I was called up to do my national service. I avoided going until I was threatened with prison if I didn't do something. Under the influence of Tippett and one of my schoolmasters, I decided to refuse. I became a conscientious objector, like Tippett, who had gone to prison during the war. I was called into the Army, but since I registered as a conscientious objector, I had to go in front of a tribunal. Most of the conscientious objectors were Quakers or other religious people, but a few were pacifists, which I claimed to be, although I wasn't really one. There was an organization called Peace Pledge Union where I was coached in order to face the tribunal, and the person who coached me was the very famous writer Vera Brittain. She prepared me to go to the tribunal in Ealing and make a case for not going into the Army. Unlike Tippett, I was willing to do alternative service, such as agriculture, coal mining or hospital work. At the hearing I was asked that if I had been a bit older during the war and been called up, would I have refused to go into the army then? Because I was trying to be honest, I said that I would have gone into the army then, but I didn't want to go in now as I am here precisely trying to avoid such situations. The tribunal consisted of trade union officials, political people, and priests, and they accepted my declared status with the provision that I would do alternative service.

By another coincidence, at the time I was working for Schott Music Publishers as an office boy. My father thought I might make a good publisher, and Universal Editions' Alfred Kalmus wanted to train me to be his successor, so I worked in Great Marlborough Street at Schott and lived with my maternal grandparents who had moved to North London in 1939. I joined up with the socialist Zionists, who had a farm in Essex where they were training people to go out and work in the kibbutz collective settlements in Israel, which was then only two years old. They suggested I go and live and work at the Essex farm, which I did, and it had an important influence on me as an alternative socialist education of sorts. I worked on the farm as a "mass murderer," killing a hundred chickens once a week, sometimes turkeys and ducks too, which doesn't seem very appropriate for one who was a conscientious objector!

I worked on the farm for a year, and then the Zionist organization sent me to Manchester to teach Marxism. In the land of the blind the one-eyed man is king, and I didn't know so much, but I probably knew a bit more than the people I was teaching. Also in Manchester I first worked in a mental hospital, and then became a ward orderly in a conventional medical hospital where I finished out my two years of national service. I worked the night shift a lot, which was an experience for a conscientious objector as many of the patients were ex-soldiers.

While working in the hospital in Manchester, I wrote my first music that was performed, a Zionist pageant. My father, who finally realized that I might be seriously interested in music, got in touch with Iso Elinson, a Russian pianist who lived in Manchester and taught at the Royal College of Music. He asked him to recommend a teacher for me, and that's how I got to Richard Hall, who I began private lessons with in 1952 when my national service ended.

## 2. RICHARD HALL AND THE ROYAL MANCHESTER COLLEGE OF MUSIC

*JVZ: Goehr and I talked about the beginning of his journey to become a composer as a student of Richard Hall's at the Royal Manchester College of Music (now known as the Royal Northern College of Music). There he met fellow students who became his lifelong friends, Peter Maxwell Davies and Harrison Birtwistle, and the three of them, along with other student friends, including pianist John Ogdon and trumpeter and conductor Elgar Howarth, formed the New Music Manchester group. Goehr was the eldest and most experienced musician, and he became their leader. The three composers are sometimes referred to as the "Manchester School," but Goehr doesn't ascribe much importance to the name now. Notwithstanding that, it is remarkable how Goehr, Birtwistle, and Davies went on to become the three biggest forces of their generation in British new music, with well-established international reputations.*

*I began our conversation by asking how it was that Goehr went to Richard Hall in the first place, and what Hall was like as a composer, man, and teacher.*

AG: My father contacted the pianist Iso Elinson at the Royal Manchester College of Music (RMCM) on my behalf and he recommended Richard Hall, the Professor of Composition at RMCM. I was still working nights in the Manchester hospital, so during the end of my national service, I went to Hall for three months of private lessons at his home in Didsbury, a Manchester suburb.

Hall had an interesting mind and his looks reminded me of Delius. He was a very tall, good-looking man with an aquiline nose. Formerly an Anglican priest, he became a Unitarian minister later in life, and was a mystic in the mold of Ouspensky and Gurdjieff. He was an organist from York, and had been part of an interesting circle of people there

*Richard Hall. Courtesy of the Royal Northern College of Music*

called the British Music Society. The founding member of the Society was the professor of music at the nearby Huddersfield technical college, Eaglefield Hull, who wrote the first English language biography of Scriabin.

I mention these things because Richard Hall's musical interests as a priest were principally Scriabin and Delius. He also loved anything to do with numbers—not mathematics really, but more the idiosyncrasies of numbers—which accounted for his interest in Schoenberg. He didn't like the music particularly, but he was drawn to Schoenberg's system of twelve-tone technique.

During the war, Hanns Eisler's first wife, Charlotte Demant, had lived in Manchester with Arnold Rosé the violinist and namesake of the Rosé Quartet, the members of which had all been in the Vienna Philharmonic before Hitler and the Anschluss. Rosé and Demant were friends of Hall's and he was very influenced by them.

I was a precocious "boy" of twenty when I started studying with Hall and thought I had the answer to every question and knew everything one needed to know. He gently deflated me in a very ironic way and made me see that whatever it was I was spouting was all second-hand stuff and didn't really add up to anything.

As I have often said, the first three months with any teacher are of crucial importance: it's when you either connect or you don't. After that, it becomes more friendly and social. The real influence comes at the beginning of the relationship. To begin with, Hall showed me how, if you take a simple pentatonic scale and you create a series of chords built up from each scale tone with every other tone—C D E G A is the scale, first chord C E A, second D G C, and so on—you can easily create a system of harmony. It's of a very simple kind, but it always sounds well and it generates a systematic process. He equated this with how we use a major or minor scale in harmonizing each note in the same way.

Ex. 1. Pentatonic scale with harmonic derivations

My teacher set me to work writing little pieces using this concept, and I remember the first one was a piano composition that I called "Carousel." He thought it was a terrible title and told me to change it, which I did. Then, after the first piece, I combined this pentatonic scale with the other common one, the one that uses only sharps—all the black keys on the piano. After a very short time I was working with ten notes, five and five. At the beginning of my efforts I was juxtaposing them— first of all a section in white notes, then a section in sharps. Then I started combining the two pentatonic scale versions, writing little pieces with ten notes, so it wasn't tonal or atonal, but something based on the combined harmony. It was quite primitive in a way and I can't remember if I discovered this process myself, or if Hall led me there. This was different from what I had been composing before, which really had no method in it. In fact, this technique played a very big part in my composition later on.

After my three months of private lessons with Hall in Manchester, I was meant to go to Oxford, where I had a scholarship to study classics. However, I didn't really want to go, so he suggested that I stay and that he would get the Oxford scholarship transferred for me to study with him at the Royal Manchester College of Music, which I did. So in 1952, I enrolled in the RMCM composition class, which was a three-year program.

The class was quite casual, and as it wasn't a degree program, you could do what you wanted. There were six to eight of us in the class doing composition in various styles and idioms. We each had a regular private lesson with Hall, then once a week we had a class where we looked at music, printed articles, and each other's pieces. Hall was a very tolerant and illuminating man, but was easily bored, so that in the private lesson, where I was meant to do harmony and counterpoint, we didn't do too much of either. A lot of time was spent with him showing me his pieces, and me showing him mine and him commenting. It was a very good experience that I learned a lot from.

In the class, we ranged far and wide in our studies. A big influence at that time, connected with the pentatonic method, was the work of Ernst Krenek. Hall was very interested in the link between modality and the twelve-tone technique. In this, he was more influenced by Josef Matthias Hauer than Schoenberg. Hauer wrote a book, *Zwölftontechnik*, that explains his ideas about getting modes out of the total twelve-tone chromatic scale. Hauer was the first to propose this method, but it was Krenek who used it in his composition. One of his pieces utilizing this method that we looked at in depth was the *Lamentations of the Prophet Jeremiah*. If you look at the preface of that piece, there is an introduction by Krenek where he shows how he derived pseudo-medieval modes out of the twelve-tone technique. He extracted two six-note modes (hexachords) and used them to create a work that has a kind of medievalism about it. That was a great influence on me. Interestingly, Krenek was very friendly with Stravinsky, and Krenek's method in this particular piece became one of the bases for Stravinsky's "rotation" technique in his late twelve-tone works.

After Hauer and Krenek, the person with the greatest influence on the Manchester College was Ferruccio Busoni. Egon Petri, Busoni's pupil, had taught in Manchester for a while, as indeed had Wilhelm Backhaus, the other great pianist of that time, and most of the piano teachers, including mine, had been pupils of Petri. Busoni was also interested in the kind of ideas we found in Hauer and Krenek, as shown in his book, *Sketch of a New Esthetic of Music*. So it was Hauer, Krenek, Busoni, and Schoenberg who I was quite interested in, and who became the influences on the culture of the Manchester class.

The Henry Watson Library at Manchester had bought an enormous number of Busoni scores which you couldn't find anywhere else. When I wasn't in class or working on something, I was in the library studying these scores and a great number of other books, including one on quarter-tones and other microtonal scales (though I could not hear those notes nor did I have any idea how to use them). These books and score studies were important from a theoretical point of view, but the big influence on us, in terms of the practicality of composing, was Hindemith, who was much performed then.

In the 1920s and 1930s, Richard Hall had worked with unemployed workers in Manchester making bamboo pipes with a cork mouthpiece that played seven or eight notes, which was the training instrument that was the predecessor of the recorder. Hall would write what he considered to be twelve-tone pieces for groups of these pipes. The pieces were very simple and, as I say, the ethos was of Hindemith—a practical kind of music-making rather than avant-garde. This concept of practicality was very much part of Hall's teaching, and the pieces we wrote to be played at the college tended to be of a practical nature. The interest in sonority that later became a big thing in modern music, we knew nothing about then; we were only interested in structure.

Hall's concert music had English folksong origins, but he treated the traditional material polyphonically and his pieces incorporated his interest in numerical systems. His pieces often used a modified dodecaphonic system, more like Krenek's music than Schoenberg. I particularly remember hearing a piece for string orchestra that was played by the Hallé Orchestra.

One of the interesting things about Richard Hall's teaching was that it was very speculative. Many kinds of musical ideas were explored in the class. I wouldn't characterize these explorations as experimental; they were more searching in character. Later, Olivier Messiaen's music came into our class "club" of influences, as his use of "modes" fit into this mentality very well. We were also introduced to the work of Joseph Schillinger because Hall knew all about his books and was attracted to their mathematical nature. Hall was as interested in all speculative music as he was bored by the conventional. However, we did analyze the music of nineteenth-century composers such as Brahms, and also studied Renaissance music.

After a year or so, Harrison "Harry" Birtwistle joined the class, though he was then technically a student at the Northern College in Manchester. He was a good clarinetist, and while he was sketching a little, he wasn't yet composing. At about the same time, Peter Maxwell "Max" Davies came to the Manchester College as a piano student of Iso Elinson's wife, Hedwig Stein.

Harry and Max came to the composition class sometimes, though I think they were far less receptive of Richard Hall than I was. They didn't see anything particular in it that was of use to them, whereas later on, after I had studied with Messiaen, been to Darmstadt and started my career as a composer, I developed what was called my "modal serialism"—where I divided the twelve-tone row into two six-note modes—which was closely related to the pentatonic harmonic technique that I learned when I was first studying with Hall. All the pieces I wrote from my *Two Choruses, op. 14* and *Little Symphony, op. 15*, up to *Metamorphosis/Dance, op. 36*, utilized this technique that I first learned from Hall and Krenek.

Ex. 2. Twelve-tone row with harmonic derivations (from *Chaconne for Winds, Op. 34*)

Of course the other composer who used these ideas was Milton Babbitt, who later became a very close friend of mine.

Remarkably, Babbitt's music also came from the same stable of influences as mine: Krenek, Hauer, and Schoenberg. He also divided his twelve-tone rows into two halves and used their respective properties, though in a much more sophisticated way than Krenek. This kind of combinatoriality in composing was a very American thing, which became important to the music of a lot of composers there.

I only met Krenek in the 1950s, but by that time he had been browbeaten by Karlheinz Stockhausen into becoming a "Darmstadt" disciple. Krenek was very intelligent and sophisticated and he wrote some very good pieces, but his best music was from earlier in his career and I don't have much interest in his later music, though I thought his *Symphonic Elegy*, written for string orchestra in memory of Webern, was a very good piece. (It was on the B side of Mitropoulos's recording of Schoenberg's *Erwartung*, which I grew up on.) I think Krenek believed that he had to go with whatever the avant-garde of the time was, but it didn't really suit him in my opinion. However, it is worth noting again that his influence on Stravinsky's late compositional style was very important.

In Richard Hall's class, Messiaen's book *Technique of My Musical Language* was much read and imitated. His modes related exactly to Hall's kind of thinking. Hall came across Messiaen because he was an organist and he played the earlier Messiaen organ pieces. We didn't know any of Messiaen's newest pieces, but mostly the piano works *Vingt Regards* and *Visions de l'amen*.

Then, in 1953, my father conducted the first British performance of *Turangalîla*, which blew my mind! I knew Messiaen wasn't a trivial composer because we had studied his older pieces and his techniques, but *Turangalîla* made an enormous impression on me. It is a truly remarkable work.

My fellow students Harry Birtwistle and Max Davies attended my father's *Turangalîla* performance with me. Max's first acknowledged piece, the *Sonata for Trumpet*, was very influenced by that experience. Elgar "Gary" Howarth, who was at Manchester University and who played the trumpet in the first performance of Max's piece, was also at my father's *Turangalila* performance. Gary was a pretty good composer too, but he didn't have any confidence in his work. He was, however, an excellent musician and went on to a long career as a conductor.

After the performance of *Turangalila* in London, we all went off to an after-concert party at the house of music critic Felix Aprahamian. Messiaen came with Yvonne Loriod, who proceeded to play Pierre Boulez's second sonata. While she played, something happened to make her fingers bleed, perhaps a paper cut from turning the pages, and by the time she finished, there was blood all over the keys of the piano. Her performance and the piece blew everyone away, and I remember leaving the party thinking that what I wanted to do was to compose music that would make someone's fingers bleed, just like Boulez!

We also looked at Boulez at that time, the first two piano sonatas, the flute *Sonatine*, and *Soleil des eaux*. We also heard some other composers' pieces via poorly received German radio, but I don't remember anything in particular. My fellow student, John Ogdon, had been a pupil of Richard Hall's since the age of eight. He used to write a symphony for each class, and when our teacher would criticize it, Ogdon would fashion the score into a paper airplane and send it flying. However, John was a remarkable pianist and he could sight-read anything. He read through the first two Boulez sonatas for us, so we in the class knew them well.

While I was at Manchester, I got together with some of my fellow students and we formed a group called New Music Manchester. The group consisted of me, Harry Birtwistle, Max Davies, John Ogdon, Gary Howarth, cellist John Dow, and a few others. We put on some concerts that we paid for ourselves in a hall in the art gallery and other small venues. There was already a new music society at the college that was more Busoni-oriented, but we were trying to do more modern music.

I had been asked by the pianist Margaret Kitchin—a friend of my father's who was married to the impresario Howard Hartog—to write a piano sonata for her that became my Opus 2 (My Opus 1 song cycle with texts by Byron has been lost.) John Ogdon thought my sonata was closely modeled on the Liszt sonata. (A big influence on us at the time was Humphrey Searle's music, which displayed his great interest in both Schoenberg and Liszt.) In my sonata, Busoni and Liszt make up one line of thought, and another line owed more to the systematic group of composers we had studied. There is clearly a twelve-tone idea at the beginning that imitates the Liszt sonata in its use of dotted rhythm. As it proceeds, it is developed through a doubling technique, which is clearly derived on the one hand from Messiaen, and on the other hand from the Krenek and Richard Hall ideas. (It was on the basis of that piece that Messiaen agreed to take me as a student in his Paris class. Yvonne Loriod said that she didn't think it was particularly good but that it showed I had the instinct for composing.)

What I mean by "doubling" technique is that you double like Messiaen did, at the third or fourth. I doubled the row with added sixth or fourth chords so it's quite primitive. My father had a hand in trying to help me improve it. There is a passacaglia in the middle, which my father said got boring as it was repetitive and never transposed. He showed me how to transform it by modulation and through Schoenbergian techniques. I don't think it's too bad a piece. It had some good ideas, some of them clearly derived from Messiaen. John Ogdon recorded it and he used to play it quite a lot.

The end of this period in Manchester was marked by a now legendary concert in the Arts Council drawing room in London, in which our Manchester group was sponsored by Sir William Glock to do a concert that was under the auspices of Elizabeth Lutyens. Harry and I played a piece by her for clarinet and piano called *Valedictions*, in memory of Dylan Thomas, which we liked a lot. I became very friendly with Lutyens and admired her greatly. Harry and I used to play together a lot, but we weren't very good at counting so we used little crosses on our parts where we were supposed to meet. We played the Alban Berg pieces, the Busoni, and Milhaud's *Sonatine*. The big influence on me at this moment was the *Abîme des oiseaux* solo clarinet movement from Messiaen's *Quartet for the End of Time*. This led to my Opus 3, the *Fantasias* for clarinet and piano which I dedicated to Harry. I couldn't play them, but John Ogdon did, and they performed this piece in the London concert. They were called fantasias not because they were fantastic, but after the Purcell *Fantasias*.

My Opus 4 was *Fantasia* for orchestra, which was written about the same time as Maxwell Davies's *Alma Redemptoris Mater* for wind sextet. At the time, there was a movement, mostly emanating from the Schoenberg School, towards creating music that was without ornamentation or decoration of any kind. (Adolf Loos had said that decoration was only suitable for public lavatories.) Through the influence of Max—who had been studying Indian music (an offshoot of the *Turangalîla* performance I think) and had written his dissertation at the university on it at a time when nobody knew much about it, and also following his interest in Renaissance and medieval music—I composed my orchestral fantasia. For the first time, I numbered the length of notes from the row, and then I ornamented them in a row-derived but nevertheless free improvisatory manner. This was a similar procedure to Max's *Alma Redemptoris Mater*, and both of these pieces were very important to us as they are what led us on to our next phase of works. Max and I were discussing these techniques all the time then.

Max and Harry both lived at home during the Manchester years, but I had a flat with my girlfriend Audrey. Our flat was where all of the New Music Manchester group gathered and had discussions and parties, and we pretended to be something like the Second Viennese School! We were just kids playing a part. I was pretending to be Schoenberg, so I criticized the others and took on a leadership role. We challenged each other and had very close personal relationships, which lasted for the next ten years or so.

It was Max who brought the early music to the group. He was in the university choir where they sang medieval and Renaissance music. Max was particularly keen on the Byrd masses and *Ye Sacred Muses*. My interest in this music was more marginal then.

One thing that did interest me was a book I found in the Henry Watson Library by Robert Lachmann (1892–1939), a German ethnomusicologist who wrote *Die Musik in den tunesischen Städten*, about the music of the Jewish people on the Isle of Djerba, off the coast of Tunisia. He got them to sing their songs, and when they repeated them, they would have the same shapes but different pitch levels. This idea fed into my musical thinking and remains there to this day. I often work with shapes, but not necessarily at identical pitch levels. From Babbitt, who disliked the literal transpositions in some of Schoenberg's work, I developed a dislike for literal repetitions of material. I very much took this notion on board, and one of my later ideas that came from this source was to use a formative pedal that distorted the row shapes.

I left Manchester after the London concert, which had an effect on the course of new music in Britain subsequently, and our group broke up. I went off to Paris and Messiaen's class and to study counterpoint with Yvonne Loriod. Harry went into the army (he was in the military band playing clarinet). Max was briefly called up, but somehow managed to get himself out of it, and soon thereafter went to Rome to study with Goffredo Petrassi.

## 3. OLIVIER MESSIAEN, YVONNE LORIOD AND THE PARIS CONSERVATOIRE

*JVZ: The 1953 British premiere of Olivier Messiaen's* Turangalîla *under his father was a defining moment in Goehr's life as well as the lives of his two student colleagues, Harrison Birtwistle and Peter Maxwell Davies. Sandy Goehr decided that very night that he wanted to go to Paris and study with the French master once his time at Manchester with Richard Hall was concluded in 1955. Being awarded a scholarship to attend Messiaen's class at the Paris Conservatoire for a year was a lucky break that made this possible.*

*Goehr's time in Paris at the Conservatoire was rewarding on many levels, and it greatly affected his compositions in one way or another right up to the present. In addition to his studies with Messiaen, he came into contact with a number of other composers from that period who were to have a lasting influence on him. Of particular importance is his friendship with Pierre Boulez, which we will cover in the next chapter.*

*Goehr and I have spoken about Messiaen and his period of study in Paris frequently over the decades, usually at my goading him for information and stories about it. He has also written about this period before, but I wanted to ask him about a few aspects of it for this chapter in light of our theme.*

*I have always felt an affinity for Messiaen's music myself, and I learned much of what I know about it from Goehr and discussing various pieces with him. Goehr tells how some of his early works exhibit Messiaen's influence. I hear this influence from that time onwards, too. There are some important sonic and organizational aspects of Goehr's music, including his use of modes and cantus firmus, which are very much features of both composers' music, as, indeed, they are of mine. I am very conscious of the fact that I have benefited greatly from Goehr's "filtering" of Messiaen's teaching into me as his student, which has meant so much to me as a composer and has colored my own musical technique and thought.*

*In addition, in this chapter Goehr tells of his studying counterpoint with Yvonne Loriod (who would later become Messiaen's wife), which had a great effect on his thoughts about teaching the subject later. He also talks about his less-than-friendly encounter with Schoenberg's pupil Max Deutsch.*

*As Goehr explains in the last chapter, and at the start of this one, Messiaen was a composer of great interest to him already, as he had studied some of Messiaen's organ pieces and other early works with Richard Hall in Manchester. It's hard to imagine now, but pieces like the* Quartet for the End of Time *were only just beginning to be known then, and they were something new and exciting for young composers in the early 1950s, as they still are today.*

*For the purposes of this book, I was especially interested in hearing details of what it was like to be in Messiaen's class on a daily basis, as well as Goehr's thoughts on his teacher as an educator, and he goes into that subject and much more here.*

AG: Messiaen was already known to me when I was in Manchester. I had heard some of his earlier pieces and read his book, *Technique of My Musical Language*. Of course there were certain links between Richard Hall's modal technique and Messiaen's use of modes of limited transposition, but his music was very far out relative to what we were listening to and studying at the time. Richard Hall, being an organist, appreciated Messiaen's works for his instrument. However, until the performance in England of *Turangalîla*, conducted by my father, we only had a vague knowledge of what his music was about.

I didn't experiment with the modes of limited transposition, but the principle of doubling in Messiaen's earlier works, such as adding a line at the sixth, and his kind of passage work were influential, and I adapted these for my own use. In my *Piano Sonata, op. 2,* there is certainly the influence of Messiaen, which

*Olivier Messiaen. Photo by Laelia Goehr*

helped me fill out the harmony and keep it from becoming too austere. The piece that made the biggest impression on me was the *Abîme des oiseaux* movement from the *Quartet for the End of Time*. I had heard it by the time I was in Manchester and knew it pretty well. I liked the unison movement very much, but the clarinet solo movement really shook me, and I think you can hear the influence of it in my *Fantasias for Clarinet and Piano, op. 3*.

I knew the Berg and Busoni pieces for clarinet and piano, but I was most captivated by the sound of the Messiaen, which moved me deeply, and I still think it's a wonderful piece. There was nothing remotely like it at the time. I also really liked the very slow movements, and later on I imitated them in the second movement of my *Piano Trio, op 18*. The extremely slow music of Messiaen was miles away from anything else I had ever heard. Music like that could easily become banal, but somehow in Messiaen's hands it transcended banality. The rhythmic thinking in the *Quartet for the End of Time* was also very new.

On the night of the English premiere of *Turangalîla* in 1953, I decided that I had to go and study with Messiaen.

I managed to get a French government scholarship to go to Paris and attend Messiaen's class for a year after my course at Manchester had finished in 1955. I had no idea what it would be like, and I suppose the obvious comparison would be with somebody who was going off to study with Schoenberg. I knew he was the great modern teacher, but I didn't know what he did in his classes. I had already been to Darmstadt and my piano sonata had been played there, so I thought I had a flavor of what to expect. As it turned out, my expectation that it would be a great avant-garde class was well off the mark!

When I first got the scholarship, my intention, which is typical of me, was to have studied with Max Deutsch, who was from the original Schoenberg class. The study with Messiaen was in a class, and part of the scholarship was to have paid for one-on-one lessons from someone else. I thought I would go and get the Max Deutsch Schoenbergian style of teaching and also attend the Messiaen class, typically trying to combine the uncombinable! I went to Deutsch and explained that I was in Messiaen's class. He was a very imposing figure, somewhat egocentric and rather grand, and he threw me out. He said anyone who wanted to study in the Schoenbergian manner does not accept any compromise, and what I was doing was a compromise.

All my life has been a compromise, and I believe in it. But Schoenberg didn't think so. "Compromise" is a word that has certain negative connotations, but I suppose what I was looking for, going back to what I picked up at home, was synthesis. I wanted to put things together that had never *been* put together, and I saw it as synthesis, not as compromise.

Deutsch wouldn't take me as a student on that basis. In fact, he wrote a very nasty letter to his former wife in London about my visit to him, which had a great effect on me. The letter said something to the effect that: "Young Goehr came to see me. He's clearly a very talented person and will doubtless make a very great career in the Darmstadt world of Stockhausen and company, with electronic music and so forth. But what he actually needs to do is to learn counterpoint properly, which is not evident in the pieces he showed me."

I was deeply offended because I was the last person who considered himself a Darmstadt camp follower, or a camp follower of any kind of music. So I thought the letter to be unfair and offensive, and I felt wounded, even though he was a much older man. But it had a great effect on me because it made it clear to me that I wasn't going to be a Darmstadt "groupie," an idea I completely rejected. I went to Darmstadt three times, and engaged with the composers who were there—Pousseur, Nono, etc.—and got very friendly with some of them, predominantly with Boulez in Paris, but I wasn't just going to be one of them, and I never have been. I did say at the time, after reading Deutsch's letter, that I wasn't exactly a supporter of what went on in Darmstadt, but I preferred talking to them than talking to you!

In fact, going to Paris created a crisis. We had made a big noise in Manchester with our new music group, but when I got to Paris I realized I wasn't quite as developed as I thought I was. There were only three of us in the class who were foreigners, the maximum number because of the laws of the Conservatoire. The rest were French students who had worked hard to be there in their final year.

When I first came to the class, I told Messiaen that I thought I should study counterpoint. He recommended that I take lessons from pianist Yvonne Loriod (who became his wife in 1961), and I went to her every week for a year to do species counterpoint and fugue. I sweated blood and it was very hard going. Up to that time I thought that the way to study counterpoint was to read all the various books on its

*Yvonne Loriod. Photo by Laelia Goehr*

history and theory. But Loriod wasn't interested in theories of counterpoint. At that time Knud Jeppeson and others were trying to introduce a historical dimension into counterpoint studies, but in Paris, they hadn't heard about this and I was required to study the subject according to the rules of the Conservatoire, which was a fixed traditional course that didn't necessarily relate to any actual musical compositions. They weren't correct in that thinking, but the valuable lesson I learned was that it wasn't talking about counterpoint that was important, but it was *doing* counterpoint that was.

Doing the species exercises, having them corrected by Loriod, and then fixing the corrections, was what was required. Loriod was very tough. It wasn't a joke! I had to do it every week, and I remember once saying to her if this is what a composer has to do then I don't think that I can do it. I learned that one can do it only very moderately at best.

Loriod was very nice to me and encouraging, but her red pencil marked a lot of faults. I hated doing the corrections, but that's what she was interested in. First make the corrections, and then do a new exercise. It was all about pushing notes around, and that's what I had avoided at Manchester where Richard Hall didn't make us do it.

This is what professional training is and a young composer has to do it. What I mainly learned from Yvonne Loriod but didn't understand until much later, was that the essence of composition lies in correcting one's work in the interest of improving it. It didn't matter whether the rules of the Conservatoire related to any actual music or not. What mattered was the relationship between student and teacher. The teacher used the red pencil and crossed out mistakes and pointed out what was inadequate. Partly it was common mistakes like parallel and direct fifths and octaves, repetition of pitches on strong beats, and boring phrases which didn't go anywhere, etc. The rule was to then do the minimum amount of correction to make it acceptable to the teacher, which sometimes means abandoning the whole exercise and rewriting it completely—but it is in the rewriting that you learn something. Later on I realized, especially after I read through English composer Thomas Attwood's exercises that he had made for his teacher Mozart with Mozart's corrections, that this *is* composition teaching.

Messiaen's class met three times a week, each four hours long. It was quite something to sit with the great man for twelve hours a week! It wasn't actually a composition class, and a lot of what Messiaen did was disappointing to me then (I was surely conceited). At the first class we looked at Beethoven's Fifth Symphony, and Messiaen said to me: "Monsieur Goehr (he addressed everyone formally), what is the form of the first movement?" I thought to myself, "My God, here I am in the presence of this great man, and I have come all the way to Paris, and the first question he asks is about Beethoven's Fifth Symphony. The answer must be miles beyond anything I know or could experience." So I said nothing. Then he asked one of the French students, who said, "Sonata form with two subjects," which met with the approval of Messiaen, who then said: "Let's go on to the next movement now."

I was into Schoenberg's motivic analysis as well as Schenker, and was absolutely flabbergasted by the sheer primitiveness of this. That side of Messiaen was very off-putting to me. We dealt with standard classics a great deal—Wagner, Beethoven, Mozart particularly, Bach, Monteverdi—and maybe I was being patronizing and foolish, but most of what Messiaen said struck me as quite silly at the time.

So, how do I feel about it now? I can tell a story that puts perspective on this question. In one class we were studying the Mozart G Minor Symphony, sitting around a table with Messiaen at one end, and we took it in turns to parse, as one does in a class. When my turn came, he asked me, "M. Goehr, tell me what happens in the next passage." I analyzed it, saying something about this chord and that motive, and so forth—nothing very sophisticated—until I came to a chord which I said was a subdominant minor. And he said: "No, M. Goehr." And I looked again and it clearly was a subdominant minor, and so I said, "It looks to me, *maître*, like a subdominant minor." "No, M. Goehr," he said. A third time I didn't contradict him and I remained silent. And he said, "The correct answer is that, at this moment, a shadow passes over the music." At the time, it struck me as ridiculous, but now, sixty years later, I think I see that he meant that anybody can tell what chord name it is, according to academic harmonic theory, but what is harder to describe is what effect it makes. Unfortunately, I was much too young and brash to get it then, and it took me a long, long time to understand what he was saying.

I have said before that the effective relationship between teacher and student is very quick; you either get something immediately or you don't get it—ever. Now, when I look back on it, and I look on the first few months with Messiaen, what stands out are certain things which I learned about him, and also what I learned about myself.

One thing that struck me about him was that he wasn't at all interested in modern academicism and analytic theory, which I thought was the issue. Messiaen was actually concerned with the physical quality of the sound and reacted to it. There were certain sounds that he liked and ones that he disliked or hated. And it was the same for durations, rhythms, numbers, etc.; he liked some and didn't like others, and he expressed himself that way. You can only really understand his work if you understand his perhaps naive and very direct attitude to sound, duration, and numbers. It never crossed my mind that some numbers were preferable to others, and it struck me that I would never be able to appreciate this, as I lacked that quality almost totally. At least consciously I could never have stood up in front of a class and said, "I like this sound but I don't like that one." I would have thought about improving and making things better, but not that. His attitude towards painting and poetry was similar. It was a very direct relationship. He didn't think it was worth reading books of any sort about music. He said they were just a conspiracy against listening!

The only book that he recommended, which I have to this day and which he was right about, was *Liber Usualis*, the Catholic collection of Gregorian chants, a book I have recommended to hundreds of my students. He said that it was the most useful book a composer could have. I have worked with that book all my life since, as have many others, including Max Davies. The interesting thing is that a composer can learn to "fake" the technique of Gregorian chant. It is not complex and you can learn it in half an hour. You can also write bogus ones, but such imitations don't make any effect, and I don't know why they don't. But that is what Messiaen was getting at all the time: the authenticity of effect. I thought of Messiaen on the one hand as being prejudiced and limited, but on the other hand there was something about him reminiscent of the painter Henri "Le Douanier" Rousseau and his mad forest scenes with wild colors. He was like that. His senses were very highly colored.

I asked Messiaen about his piece *Messe de la Pentecôte*, one of the best organ works he wrote. I couldn't find a score anywhere and when I asked him about it, he said he would loan me his copy for a few days. He brought the score to the next class for me, and to my surprise it was a printed score that was marked in his hand in considerable detail. For instance, a note said "compare *Tristan* Act II bar 725" to things he quoted. He had a repertoire of things he admired, sometimes a segment or just a small fragment of a large composition. There were certain passages that came from *Tristan* and *Boris Godunov* that he particularly favored, but he also took from works by Bach and Mozart, for instance isolating an actual chord he liked and using it in his own piece. I might use something like that as a quotation in one of my pieces and then transform it in some way, but he took the actual sounds and placed them within the context of his own music. That's pretty surprising, but the idea of it refers back to his concerns with the physicality of sound.

We did a lot of ear training in the class. The pieces Messiaen used for this were often very modern pieces. He used Schoenberg's *Erwartung*, playing chords or little figures and asking us to identify them. He particularly liked *Incantations* by André Jolivet for solo flute. Jolivet had somehow been a pupil of Varèse, a composer whom Messiaen admired. (He said to me in class on one occasion, "Varèse is my brother.") He would walk to the piano from his chair and he would play what he wanted to be identified and then ask one student to tell him what it was. The French students were incredibly good at this as they had all been trained in *solfège*, which we hadn't been at Manchester. I couldn't even tell the first note, never mind what happened afterwards! I was quite good at rhythmic analysis, but couldn't do the pitches as I had had no training in it. I had reasonable relative pitch, but the French knew what notes they were, although I'm not sure whether they had absolute pitch or not.

Here is a little jokey anecdote: When we were talking about Debussy's *Pelléas and Mélisande*, which we spent quite a lot of time on, Messiaen would get up, go to the piano, play a chord, and say, "What is this chord?": i.e., name it. I had observed that he tended to favor particular chords. Once, as he stood up to go to the piano, he said, "M. Goehr, what is this chord?" and before he could play it on the piano, I told him what it was! Messiaen was very surprised and asked me, "How did you know?" I said, "*Maitre*, you particularly favor that chord!" I suppose this incident illustrates my own attitude to music, the limitations of my own ear and my effort to try and understand things in some other way.

The big work of his that was performed during that year was *Oiseaux exotiques*, which is a masterpiece. He normally never talked about his own work, but in the weeks preceding the premiere of the new piece, we asked him whether he would tell us something about it. He always brought lots of books to class, and the next class he came with a particularly large heap of books, all of which had pictures of birds. He sat down at the piano, and said the name of a bird, like *le merle noir*, the blackbird, and he would then refer to his own notes and play the songs of that bird—which he had notated—on the piano. Later on I realized that what he was doing was explaining what his piece was about, and it was just that and nothing else. The only other elements in it which he included in his bird compositions were passages based on the landscape in which the birds sang, and those had a different sort of construction.

At the time, I had never taken any interest in birds at all. I made a joke and said I felt that a bird should be employed by the

Conservatoire to teach twelve-tone technique to the students, and this remark and others like it were not appreciated by my teacher. He said, "M. Goehr, with your silly giggling, I'll not take you to the forest to listen to the birds because the birds would be disturbed and fly away."

He admired anything Asian, and he especially liked Chinese things. Once each term the class went to a Chinese restaurant, a touristy place in the Champs-Élysées that was not very good. It didn't really have anything very Chinese, and we ate things like chop suey. (I had eaten somewhat more sophisticated Chinese food in restaurants in London and Manchester.) As we sat around the table, Messiaen told us with each mouthful that we ate, to see how many tastes we could indentify separately (this was a sort of composition lesson). The best person at this was his favorite pupil, the Canadian composer Gilles Tremblay.

I certainly wasn't a favorite pupil, and I was regarded as a sort of alien element, I suspect. Messiaen had pupils who were very much influenced by him and who imitated him. I was not one of those. Once or twice during the term, you could ask to show him a piece. After the four-hour class, if you had an appointment, you would stay behind and meet him privately. He would read your score and comment on it. I showed him my orchestral piece, *Fantasia, op. 4*, which was going to be performed at Darmstadt that year. He looked quite carefully at my score, one page after another. Then he said, "Pardon me, but I wouldn't be able to write like this." I was deeply shocked because the idea that this great man would say he wouldn't write like me struck me as ridiculous. But before I could settle into *feeling* ridiculous, he pointed to the score and said, "This passage here could have been done in a slightly different way," and suddenly I was brought back down to earth with a bump. I realized that he actually knew more about it than I thought!

Messiaen was very keen on talking about literature in a class which was called "The Philosophy of Music"—a rather pretentious name for it. The philosophical element came from one or two French philosophers. Gaston Bachelard was a favorite, and he recommended that we buy all of his books. I didn't because, firstly, I had no money, and secondly, his writings about the flight of birds and things like that I didn't consider to be real philosophy. At the time I was interested in Karl Marx, not the philosophy of bird flight.

Messiaen was also interested in the Catholic poet and playwright Paul Claudel, and, surprisingly, Paul Eluard, who was a communist. You must remember that Messiaen was a devout Catholic and had no idea about politics, while half the students were members of the Communist Party. Although everyone was very discreet, this had an effect on the way things were talked about.

All of the writers, philosophers, and painters Messiaen was interested in were French, and nothing came from the outside world. I got the impression from him that there was little "outside." At that time, London would have been as near to him as Timbuktu is to us (though later on he worked in London and was there a lot). He had no idea what was going on outside France and had a very restricted view. France of that time was still in the postwar period and was very different from what it is today.

The musicians that Messiaen most often mentioned were his teachers Paul Dukas, whom he often quoted and was very influenced by, and Maurice Emmanuel, who was interested in music theory as well as composition. Otherwise it was Milhaud and Jolivet that he talked about. As for Schoenberg and Stravinsky, he only liked Schoenberg in the atonal period, and he hated the twelve-tone works and thought they were terrible. He liked Stravinsky only up to *Le Sacre du printemps*, and his analysis of this piece's rhythmic cells is not that far from the published analysis by Boulez. (He was very interested in finding rhythmic cells in music.) Later works by Stravinsky didn't interest him at all. He hated them, and he disliked Poulenc as well. He did say that he liked Alban Berg. Oddly, he never talked about Villa Lobos, who I later found out he was friends with and who had a considerable influence on the style of *Turangalîla*. He admired Milhaud and Honegger the most of the composers of that time. He didn't talk about Satie at all and didn't appear to know anything about Scriabin, whose music is in some ways comparable to his own.

Most importantly, it was Mussorgsky, Wagner, Debussy, and Ravel who really interested him. We spent a lot of time on *Gaspard de la nuit* and Messiaen did a very good analysis of it. He was also interested in what was then called "folk music," but mostly it wasn't authentic. His information came from some rather feeble Conservatoire handbooks on folk songs that consisted of things such as so-called Peruvian melodies with added piano accompaniments, as was the custom of that time. Sometimes he would quote these literally and make us sing them. Whether they were really Peruvian, there is no way of knowing. It was in the days when there wasn't any such thing as ethnomusicology in Paris and no one knew anything at all about it. (There was also the encyclopedia of the Conservatoire, where you could find all the theories of Indian rhythms that Messiaen used.)

While I can now say that the lessons seemed pretty primitive and theoretical, this is not important, because, like my counterpoint studies, they resulted in exercises that I had to do. Messiaen was very interested in teaching Greek poetic rhythms: dactyl, spondees, iambics, etc., and then constructing strophes out of them. There was a late Renaissance composer he admired very much, Claude Le Jeune, who wrote in Greek meters. Something he suggested that we do and that I still do sometimes, is that we compose theoretically out of rhythms—say, dactylic pentameter, long-short-short—that you repeated, but the last time you cut off one of the short notes to get a caesura: long-short-short, long-short. Messiaen thought that you could then introduce variation by changing durations: long-short-short, a whole note, then two half notes, after which one of the notes could be dotted as a variation.

We composed quite complicated theoretical models ourselves with variation techniques based on models that he used in his work, like adding dots regularly instead of simple augmentation and diminution. I have often done this and I sometimes still do it. You can find that the real source of this is in Messiaen's piece *Livre d'orgue*, which I think is the greatest of all his pieces. I also like the *Quatre Études de rythme*, especially the *Mode de valuers d'intensités*, and as a purely musical experience, the *Neumes rythmiques*. I think they are little masterpieces and contain several technical devices that I have adapted and imitated in many ways. Also, I love Messiaen's best orchestral piece, *Chronochromie*, from 1960, which also uses these techniques. For me, that's his great period, and these are the pieces I really go back to.

I didn't really have a relationship with Messiaen after the class. I kept my distance and from time to time I paid my respects. I would greet him at concerts and correspond with him occasionally, and I dedicated a piece to him. When he wrote letters to me, he wrote by hand. In the years that followed it took me a long time until I had learned to appreciate what I got from his class. For many years I was quite cynical and blasé about it. I don't normally like camp followers who are too close to somebody; in that sense I didn't like the Schoenberg, Hindemith, Messiaen, or Stockhausen followers. I have always been independent, and in that case perhaps I am naturally perverse. (You name it, and I don't agree!)

What Messiaen said to me during that year of study certainly changed my attitude towards music altogether, permanently. I completely understand it today, but at the time I didn't realize what it was all about because I had my own agenda which was quite different. I didn't know any of this until I looked back on it years later. My wanting to study with Max Deutsch while in the Messiaen class was because of the urge for synthesis within me. At that time, there was the Stravinsky camp and the Schoenberg camp, and it was said you had to choose. My father found that patently ridiculous and managed to admire both, and that had an effect on my thinking too. You have to appreciate that it's all beautiful music!

## 4. PIERRE BOULEZ

*JVZ: Like Schoenberg, Pierre Boulez has loomed over Goehr's music for most of his life, as Goehr explains in this chapter. He first became aware of the older composer as a student in Manchester, and as he described in the previous chapter, he first heard Boulez's music performed live the night that Yvonne Loriod played his Second Piano Sonata at the party in London after Walter Goehr's U.K. premiere of Messiaen's* Turangalîla. *The two young composers were to meet later in Paris during Goehr's study with Messiaen at the Conservatoire, and they formed a quick friendship which was quite close for a number of years.*

*Boulez and Goehr had a complicated relationship after the 1950s, which sometimes took the form of public and private dialogues expressing admiration as well as differences of opinion on aesthetics, compositional mechanics, and other matters. These discussions were fascinating to me as a student and remain so today. You can get a flavor of this by reading Goehr's 1987 lecture, "A Letter to Pierre Boulez," reprinted in his collected writings,* Finding the Key. *I believe the last time Boulez conducted a premiere of one of Goehr's works was the* Chaconne for Winds, op. 34, *with the BBCSO in 1975.*

*I first met Boulez when I was Goehr's assistant in the late 1970s, introduced to him by Goehr at a dress rehearsal for a Prom concert in the Royal Albert Hall where Boulez was conducting the BBCSO in a premiere of a work by Harrison Birtwistle. I sat behind Harry looking at his score during the rehearsal, and was privy to his fascinating conversation with Boulez about various aspects of the rehearsal of his piece after the first run-through. Of course, this was a huge moment and an eye-opening experience in my young life. I was lucky enough to speak with Boulez a few more times over my younger years, and found him kind and softly spoken, with an aura of self-assured energy that was unique in my experience.*

*It is well known that Boulez had a piercing, ferocious intellect and was very opinionated and upfront about what he thought (often brutally so), what music he liked, and especially what he didn't like. Goehr and I have discussed Boulez and his work innumerable times from when I was a student right up to the present. Boulez was arguably the biggest figure in their generation of European and American postwar composers and was hugely influential on all of them, owing somewhat to the "Darmstadt effect." Composers of my generation who began their careers in the early 1970s were also very much affected by Boulez's work and its theoretical/aesthetical influence, and it was something that we all had to come to terms with, one way or another. For me, Boulez was and still is a very important figure, mostly as a result of my studying and absorbing his works and writings, but as a reaction to them as well.*

*There is no doubt about Boulez's position as an important mentor to the younger Goehr, but I also sense the essence of it lingering in the recesses of his entire catalog, as does the influence of Messiaen, Hall, Eisler, Walter Goehr, and the rest of the mentors discussed in this book. It's all part of who Goehr is and what his music is. Consequently, all of them exert an influence on my own music because of it, especially Boulez in my case. I think the jury is still out on Boulez's music after the 1950s and 60s, and it may be many decades before our music culture completely comes to terms with it. However, as Goehr has said, "Boulez's failures are better than most composers' successes."*

AG: As I have said on many occasions, I believe that, for the most part, the period of time when a teacher or mentor has an influential relationship with a young composer is short and typically compressed into a time span of a few months. This was certainly the case between me and Pierre Boulez, who I spent quite a lot of time with early in my professional life in the late 1950s and early 60s. I went on knowing him less and less over the years, to the point of politeness and friendliness,

*Alexander Goehr with Pierre Boulez, late 1950s. Goehr Archive*

but nothing more, and he stopped conducting my pieces quite a long time ago.

The name of Boulez became known as one of the standard bearers of avant-garde music in the postwar period.

I first became aware of him around 1952. The pieces that I heard first were the first two piano sonatas and the flute sonatine, and I heard broadcasts of *Le soleil des eaux* and *Le visage nuptial* in their original Radio France versions. The first time he came to my notice would have been in Richard Hall's class when we read the essays (in French—it was only much later they were translated into English) published at that time. The essay I found most interesting then was "*Eventuellement*," ("Eventually" in the English version of *Notes of an Apprenticeship*), which is a speculative article about different techniques, some of which he had already applied, and some that had potential for the future, such as *bloc sonore*, etc. That article had a profound influence on me. I had no idea what he stood for or what kind of a person he was, but I thought of him as a leader of serial music. I formed no clear idea about the man, but I did have a visual picture of his music which was printed early on by Heugel.

That graphic music notation "picture" was the thing that struck me, especially of the Second Sonata, but also the flute *Sonatine* and First Piano Sonata. Peter Maxwell Davies described these scores as looking like "Clapham Junction!" The pieces consisted of incredibly complex polyphony which I wouldn't have been able to make heads or tails of, though I would have probably picked up the overall form of it. Gradually, as I learned the theory of it, I began to understand what it was and its relationship to total serialism, i.e., to what was to become *Structures* for two pianos. I became aware of all of this in a very vague but profound way while I was at Manchester, long before I really heard Boulez's music performed live or met him. The first time I actually heard any of his music in person was the time I mentioned when Yvonne Loriod played his Second Sonata at a private party the evening after my father conducted the English premiere of Messiaen's *Turangalîla*. That performance by Loriod made an enormous impression on me. As I said, I was a Busoni follower in Manchester, and the sheer pianism implied by the Boulez Second Sonata score fascinated me, even though I had no understanding of it. I didn't try to analyze it, I just heard the sounds. It was a wild experience and I realized at the time that it was nothing ordinary.

I can't remember the first time I met Boulez, but it might have been one of the times he came to the Conservatoire at the end of the class to tell Messiaen something. Or it might have been at a concert. Anyway, I very quickly formed a relationship with him. Boulez was very generous and he would invite me and my fellow British student, John Carewe, up to his small flat to talk about "modern music." John and I went to see him a dozen times or more where he had lived since his father had sent him at the age of sixteen to occupied Paris from his home in the south of France. He had rented two adjoining *chambres de bonne* in the Rue Beautreillis in the Marais district in 1945. They were actually very small maid's rooms, but he had a tiny kitchen and bath. I remember there were books and a small piano in the tight quarters, and John and I would go there for two hours or so on each visit.

We talked very broadly about Webern, Varèse, Stravinsky up to *The Rite of Spring*, and Schoenberg up to *Jakobsleiter* and the First World War (a Darmstadt-type conversation). Carewe and I were more oriented to Schoenberg because of my father, and we argued quite fiercely with Boulez. At this time, he was very hostile to the Schoenberg follower René Leibowitz, who had also been his teacher, and he had parted ways in very bad grace from him.

Boulez was really against Leibowitz, and his opposition to Schoenbergian twelve-tone music partly originated in his quarrel with him. Nobody quite knows what the feud was about. Boulez had left Messiaen with a group of other students, including his contemporaries, Jean-Louis Martinet and Serge Nigg (an interesting man whom I got to know later).

They deserted Messiaen in the late forties to go to Leibowitz, and then something went wrong. Leibowitz was a considerable character who I had a lot of admiration for as a theorist, composer, and conductor. He was an interesting man, a Pole who had been in the French resistance and a pupil of Ravel's (not Schoenberg or Webern, as some have claimed). He was good friends with Sartre, who actually wrote an introduction to one of Leibowitz's books. If you compare the Boulez essays with the books by Leibowitz of the time about Schoenberg's school and the twelve-tone technique, you find that Boulez and Leibowitz's essays overlap considerably. What Leibowitz was that Schoenberg wasn't was a defender of the idea of polyphony as being the salient aspect of music, which is something that Boulez obviously took from him.

Whatever the rift was about, it was deep. I once went with Boulez to a concert where Leibowitz was conducting an orchestra in a performance of Schubert's Fifth Symphony, and Boulez was very cynical about how Leibowitz had taken the dotted rhythms of the last movement as triplets, long-short, long-short (crotchet-quaver), etc. Boulez gave this as an example of Leibowitz's incompetence and inexactitude. Of course, Leibowitz was completely correct because it is supposed to be played like that! Even years later, after Boulez had got older and was very courteous and polite, if you mentioned Leibowitz, the old Boulez, the stormy one, immediately reappeared. It seems that Boulez killed Leibowitz's career.

Boulez was very fiery when I first met him. There was a "divine fury" in his composition, in him, and in his opposition to people he didn't like. He was a tempestuous figure, but later on that disappeared, at least from view.

I admired the stormy figure that I first knew in the 1950s. The sessions that we had, which included a lot of laughing at people we didn't approve of, were actually the source of my great affection and admiration for him. We sometimes went to concerts together. I remember once going to a performance of a piece by the Greek composer Mikis Theodorakis who was quite fashionable at the time and later famous for composing a lot of left-wing songs. It was a passacaglia that was performed, not a bad piece, but it was conventional in a kind of general style (like Bartók, say) that audiences would have heard as "modern." With perfect timing, in the five seconds between the end of the piece which came with a colossal flourish, and the beginning of the applause, Boulez managed to kill the whole thing by saying "Bravo" very quietly in that momentary silence. It had a disastrous effect in that it made the piece sound even more ridiculous than it did anyway.

We argued a lot, though we were very friendly. I often disagreed with him, but always felt that I was wrong and he was right, in spite of disagreeing with him, which is the indication of a complicated relationship. I'm not sure why exactly he gave me so much of his time. I was a young composer from another country, but I had been to Darmstadt where my music had been performed, so he didn't consider me as being totally beyond the pale and thought I was a reasonable person. He was very open to talking to people. He wasn't snobbish or anything like that. He liked talking.

Later on I felt there were limits to the possibilities of disagreement with him. At times I went outside what they euphemistically call in politics a "red line" stylistically (and there were many styles and types then in Paris—Boulanger, Poulenc, and others with more admirers than Boulez had— some of it clearly beyond the pale). You had to remain within a certain type of music in order to talk to him, as I indeed did because it was what I also believed. He had two big dislikes with which I disagreed. One was his attitude to a lot of—especially German—music of the past, which he simply dismissed out of hand in a way that was customary in Paris in the 1950s. They loved Wagner, but they didn't even know who Brahms was. They admired Schumann and Chopin, but it was a very limited understanding of music compared to the background I came from. The second thing was so-called neoclassical Stravinsky and twelve-tone Schoenberg, which was loathed in Paris. I think those prejudices, which I argued with, remained with him always, although he had to conduct a lot of this music later on.

I remember once going to dinner with him after a BBC broadcast concert at Maida Vale Studio. I was waiting for him while he was conducting a Haydn symphony, the last piece of the concert. After the performance, he saw me, waved and walked straight off the rostrum towards me, without going to his conductor's room, and asked, "Are we going out?" I replied, "Aren't you a bit hot after conducting that piece?" And he replied, "Oh no! That Haydn symphony you just beat two and three, and there's nothing to it." Someone who just beats two and three in a Haydn symphony is perhaps rather limited in his understanding of it. Though he acquired a bit of polish and skill at performing them over the years, I don't think he really understood them. Indeed, he wasn't very good at conducting the Viennese classics.

I remember one discussion with him about middle-period Schoenberg. He didn't like thick chromatic chords in the bass. He liked more airy music (and why not). I said to him that he was arguing against the pieces not because of their merits as structural compositions, which he didn't seem very concerned with, but because of questions of style. I remember telling him he would end up like Vincent d'Indy, as a professor at the Conservatoire. Well the joke's on me, because that's exactly what I ended up as!

We argued about style a great deal. I think it's an intrinsically false way to assess music, yet in Boulez's case, he developed what he thought of as a style of his own.

When I would sometimes show him a piece like my string quartet that I was trying to write then, his criticism was like Yvonne Loriod's with my counterpoint exercises—that I was doing something that wasn't allowed within the "style" as he heard it. For instance, if you wrote an adjoining minor second (E-F) around middle C, the next note, whatever it was, could not be in the same octave tessitura as the previous ones. I asked, "Why do you make such a fixed principle so that you criticize other music from that point of view? What's the point of it?" He had a sort of a Palestrina kind of mentality, obviously somewhat evolved, and in answering my question he said: "To cancel out tonal expectations, because if you write E-F-A-flat above middle C, the listener will resolve the A-flat to a G and create a tonal cadence."

This leads to a huge philosophical question about the nature of tonality and how we hear things. Boulez was interested in this subject because he was trying to reimagine music in the postwar period, and the only models he had for this were Webern's works—I now think he misunderstood him, though I didn't think that then—in trying to create an abstract language of music which didn't refer at all to the music of the past.

This view had a great effect on the Darmstadt composers at the time. Take for instance Stockhausen's *Kontrapunkte*. Boulez showed me an early version of the score which had all these conjunct intervals. It looked like it had been influenced by Bartók. And he showed me how he had corrected the thing to change the octave positions of everything, so that it looks as it does now. He formed a sort of abstract style, distorting what he had written. In one passage, there is an A minor chord, and Stockhausen hadn't noticed it because he had spelled it as B-sharp, F-flat, G-double sharp, or some other enharmonic arrangement, and he hadn't realized he had written it. Boulez hadn't spotted it either and it became a joke. The rest of the piece he corrected with his minute writing in colored ink. It was this concept of a style which I was then, perhaps more naively, but still am now, deeply opposed to.

Of course, Boulez thought you had to get rid of every remnant of tonality. I set against that idea the painter Francis Bacon's remark about how if he accidentally dripped paint on a picture, he would leave it there and incorporate it into the picture, which is the opposite approach to Boulez. If you make a polyphonic structure with a tone row, say in three parts, you very often find that the vertical relationships are quasi-tonal, or they remind you of some other music. I have always thought that it is a gift from the Almighty when your music creates a nice sound by itself without any calculations! But Boulez thought it was bad, and it was something that Boulez and I argued about. My late friend Oliver Knussen called that "self-censorship." That's exactly what it is and that's something I am very much against.

There were certain things we talked and argued about which Boulez later published essays on. We went over the last movement of the Webern Second Cantata and the Schoenberg *Five Pieces for Orchestra*, and Debussy's *Jeux*. The introduction of *Jeux* is the segment of the piece that interested him the most because he thought he had discovered a kind of metric and pitch class structure which showed Debussy was well ahead of his time. It's a good introduction, but I didn't see anything particularly dramatic about it and I don't think it's what's striking about the piece. In *Jeux*, I said that after those beginning bars, it seemed to me like conventional Debussy. We argued a bit about it, and he said, "No, it isn't." (I was probably being dogmatic without knowing enough about it.) Then he went over to the piano and started playing it, then turned his head to John and me every once in a while and said, "isn't it very beautiful music, just lovely?" And in the end it's just that. There was no particular new principle observed.

We also talked about the Debussy *Études* which he admired particularly, for instance the study in fourths which was a model of his.

Boulez was a mentor to me precisely because of these kinds of arguments and disagreements, which I got a great deal out of. Even today I often think when I am composing: "What would Pierre say about that?" I know that he wouldn't have seen it if he were still alive; he wouldn't have cared because the whole context wouldn't have interested him at all. Somehow these thoughts remain with me. In fact, almost all of Messiaen's pupils who were also influenced by Boulez had a kind of attitude towards presentation of pitch that I can easily identify with. It partly has to do with his idea of style which I opposed so much, but which I am not freed from. It's not style insofar as its handwriting is inevitable. I do not believe that the concept of style should be in a composer's mind when he is creating a work, or in a writer's or a painter's either. They ought to be concerned with something outside themselves, because the personality and the "style" will emerge anyway. There is no way of avoiding it.

There is the famous Wittgenstein story where he is sitting around the table with the board of examiners for the Cambridge tripos, and every member of the board was to pose a question that would be incorporated into the exam paper. When it came to Wittgenstein, he pulled out a piece of paper from his jacket and read his question. The chairman said, "But Professor Wittgenstein, you asked the same question last year." And he said, "Yes, but the answer will be different this year." In that is the business about style.

When we do counterpoint, we all do roughly the same thing stylistically, according to given rules, etc. But if I ask a student to correct a counterpoint exercise, they will do it one way, and if I ask another student to also correct it, they won't come up with the same solutions. Sometimes they will be similar, and sometimes radically different. That's because personality and style emerge by themselves. But in order for that to be effective, you have to concentrate on the rules and the structure of what's before you. If you are too concerned with personality, and consequently with style, and ask yourself: "Am I sounding like me or am I sounding like somebody else," the "you" is already in trouble. That's bad. And that's what's wrong with a great deal of music.

The great thing of the Schoenbergian tradition was that it refocused the concern with material in a manner that earlier composers had. Boulez started like that too, but for other reasons he didn't retain it. One of the reasons relates to Mallarmé. Boulez talked a lot about Mallarmé, not about the famous poems, but he was most interested in *Le Livre*, the book by Mallarmé where the letters and words were distributed polyphonically all over the pages, along with blank spaces and empty pages. It was Mallarmé in a semi-mystical way trying to portray the world. (This book was published in its final unfinished state.)

At that time, there were various scholars who had written books about this quasi-religious attempt by Mallarmé to create this huge, abstract form. And that was the model for Boulez. Creating a *modus operandi* is the thing that I think he believed in until the day he died. It was the core of his work, and though I didn't realize it at the time because it hadn't happened yet, I now believe that quest is what limited his development. I very much admired then, as I do now, those pieces up to *Pli selon pli*. But later on, he composed with these huge structures that were never finished and became rather like Mallarmé's book. That is a great tragedy, because I do believe that he was the greatest talent of our time.

Perhaps Boulez failed in realizing his great vision on his own terms. In fact, perhaps we prefer the people who failed to those who succeeded because they are more interesting in a way. However, imposing a style on a generation of composers in Boulez's way would make everyone sound the same. There is no difference in that and what was imposed on people by authoritarian regimes. In Darmstadt, the sounding like everybody else was almost like having a party badge or a uniform. And you either wore that badge or else. I came to realize that because I didn't wear the badge.

My friend Stefan Wolpe brought this up in Darmstadt, and not to his advantage. He very clearly pointed out to them the authoritarian nature of what they were doing. I already had deep opposition to this kind of thing, partly from Wolpe and partly from Hanns Eisler, which is another side of me that we will come to later. Because Boulez led the charge on this at Darmstadt, it would be easy to describe it as egotistical or arrogance on his part. If you are a visionary and a Utopian idealist, you will probably be arrogant. You could say the same about Schoenberg. The big difference between Schoenberg and Boulez is that Schoenberg's influence is everywhere in the musical world, and Boulez's isn't, and probably won't be. Schoenberg was a great teacher, which Boulez wasn't. However, Boulez was very generous and Schoenberg less so.

When Boulez conducted my pieces, I didn't think he was particularly successful at it. We are different sorts of people and he couldn't be a conductor without being a composer, and so what he didn't like, he suppressed. The most important thing I learned from Boulez was the feeling of urgency: You have to do something. Push some notes around. A sense of urgency is a most important quality that a composer *must* have.

## 5. DARMSTADT

*JVZ: Although the annual Darmstadt Festival was obviously not a mentor or teacher as such, it did provide a unique learning experience for young Goehr in his three times attending in the 1950s. We felt that his account of what it was like, what he took from it, and his observations of the attendees and the event itself were very important to the composer he was then, as well as being a valuable insight for history. In addition, some of what he did as a composer afterwards was in many ways a reaction to the Darmstadt effect and its leading composers of the time.*

*As shown in the preceding chapter, Goehr had an important, close relationship with Boulez, arguably the prime mover of Darmstadt then. His lifetime friendship with some of the composers he met there, Luigi Nono in particular, provided him with peers to talk to about composing and compare notes with on what they were doing and how they thought. This peer-group learning experience is of great value to young composers, who are especially in need of it as they develop their careers. In addition, contact with the older generation of established composers such as Dallapiccola, Leibowitz, and Maderna was invaluable to Goehr.*

*We have often discussed the impact of the ideas that came out of Darmstadt in the 1950s on the musical culture of our time and the period in between. For Goehr and the generation of young composers that lived it, it had some kind of effect on every one of them, both positive and negative. For American and British composers of my generation who were students in the 1960s and 1970s, the kind of high modernism practiced at Darmstadt had been absorbed into the teaching and musical practice of composition of that time, and provided ideas that could be imitated, often with less than stellar results, but important as learning experiences. I remain fascinated by the techniques that came out of that time, such as integrated serialism and the conscious application of complicated mathematics and number theory to composing. These ideas have been present in my music throughout my career, though I have found my own way of using them and they remain in the deep background.*

*I have Goehr to thank for how I do use the ideas that came out of Darmstadt, as he showed me various methods of adapting and applying such ideas, and the different results these lead to. These ideas were a part of his music too, and remain so, though with a definite, unique personal stamp. This was a valuable lesson for me as his student almost fifty years ago, and I learned how to adapt musical construction techniques from any period or style for my own purposes from Goehr, who is a master of such synthesis.*

*To begin the conversation that makes up this chapter, I asked Goehr if he would relate how he came to go to Darmstadt in the first place, and to give a personal view of his experiences and observations there. I also wanted to know his reaction on looking back on it from the present with more mature eyes and ears.*

AG: I became aware of the Darmstadt Summer Courses for New Music in 1952 or '53 and went there three times. I was very nervous about going to Germany for the first time and it was a very sensitive subject at home. My mother didn't want me to go at all, but my father had been there to conduct since the War and he didn't mind.

I went to the Darmstadt Festival for the first time in 1954, when I was in my third year at Manchester. Harry Birtwistle came with me, and I remember we went on the Euro Bus and almost missed our connection in Luxembourg. The first time was very different from the other times I went. It was very pleasant and quite compelling, and I made friends with Bernd Alois Zimmermann (who never came again), Stockhausen, Pousseur, Nono, and a number of others. My Piano Sonata, op. 2 was performed there.

The most interesting composer there was Bruno Maderna. He was a wonderful musician and man, and was very broadly cultured. Maderna gave a daily seminar in which he discussed pieces that were being performed at the Festival (I remember him talking about Stockhausen's first four *Klavierstücke*, for instance). The concerts were very catholic in taste, and there were all sorts of pieces performed. The Schoenberg School was well represented, and it was the beginning of the interest in Webern.

I was, however, struck by one thing that very much offended me. René Leibowitz, whom I had met and came to know over the following years, gave a lecture in which he talked about the beginnings of the Webern cult. He said that it was impossible to understand Webern individually without reference to Schoenberg. At that point, Stockhausen and Henri Pousseur walked out noisily, slamming the door. They then went to Dr. Wolfgang Steinecke, the musicologist who was the head of the Festival, and said if Leibowitz was invited again, they would not come.

Being suspicious of things German, this shocked me, especially since I thought Leibowitz was right, and Stockhausen's and Pousseur's behavior bore the stamp of authoritarianism. It was the beginning of the cult of Webern that consisted of the idea that Webern represented a new beginning in music, and over the years that I went to Darmstadt, that point of view prevailed.

That first year I attended, lots of composers were performed: Milhaud, Bartók, Stravinsky, Messiaen, Schoenberg, and Webern. The concept behind Darmstadt was for Germany to make up for the things they hadn't heard because of the Nazis. It was to have a fairly broad perspective with all sorts of points of view, something that I wholeheartedly approved of.

In Maderna's classes we looked at scores and discussed them. Because of our studies in Manchester, we knew who Boulez was and had read some of his articles, but we hadn't heard much of his music, though John Ogdon had sight-read through the Second Piano Sonata for us. I had also heard Yvonne Loriod play the sonata at that private party after my father's premiere performance of Messiaen's *Turangalîla* in London. In Darmstadt, music by Boulez, Nono, and Maderna was performed, along with Webern, and the performances had a stimulating atmosphere and felt like something new.

Luigi Nono and I became friends, partly for political reasons. I liked him very much. He had various pieces that he explained to me. There was a ballet for orchestra after Lorca called *The Red Coat* (*Der rote Mantel*). He had the score of that piece as it was being done in Germany, and also one of his earlier pieces that was being performed at Darmstadt that year. Theodor Adorno was also there. I saw him practicing the piano, and heard him lecture, but I didn't have any conversations with him. I remember that pianist Eduard Steuermann and violinist Rudolf Kolisch came and played the Schoenberg *Phantasy*.

A division between the older and younger generation was just beginning at that time. One unfortunate casualty was Dallapiccola, who I thought very highly of, but who was ignored and not performed. Hans Werner Henze had been there in previous years, but had been excluded by 1954.

By the time I went again in 1956, when my *Fantasia for Orchestra, op. 4* was performed by the Frankfurt Radio Symphony Orchestra, the formulation of the so-called Darmstadt style and ideology had taken place, consisting of two concepts that became clear to me. The first was that music had to begin again from scratch. Year Zero was 1945. This was a reflection of literary thinking in Germany of the Group 47 association, which the more progressive German writers supported. The aim was to purify the language and get rid of its misuse during the Nazi times. This was akin to the idea of creating a new musical style from scratch—what Paul Klee would call "from the single dot."

The second Darmstadt idea called for the separation of the important music of the early twentieth century—Schoenberg, Webern, Berg, Stravinsky, Bartók—into progressive and residual traditional categories. The point was to get rid of the residual traditional works, and emphasize the creation of a progressive canon. This would have come from Boulez, who promoted a mixture of those two elements. For instance, nothing by Stravinsky after *The Rite of Spring* and *Les Noces* was considered of any interest whatsoever (which to a certain extent reflected the views of both Messiaen and Boulez), as well as nothing of Schoenberg's after his unfinished *Jakobsleiter* of 1918 (which had its first performance around this time). Schoenberg's twelve-tone works were declared unacceptable as they were considered to be "neoclassical," and that was a dirty word (and still is among some people), and they didn't want to hear this music at all.

Webern was isolated as the leader of the school, which goes completely against the nature of what Webern had done. It ignored the fact that Webern wrote in variation and sonata forms and was deeply embedded in tradition. At Darmstadt, they didn't want to know that because this was the time of the "single note." They perceived Webern's music purely as polyphony of pitches, durations, and dynamics, and tried to analyze it regardless of any motivic or semantic content. They pointed to the dislocated nature of these things, and what's more, they performed Webern's pieces like that. These performances were basically false. Now we have the very good recordings of Webern, but at that time there were few recordings of his music and none of them were very good. However, in postwar Germany, of course, this was something new.

The important point is that these aspects contributed to what the word "Darmstadt" signifies today, i.e., a kind of didactic formalism made up of different musical aspects that were considered progressive: Stravinsky in rhythm, Schoenberg in freedom of tonality and expressionism, Varèse in sonority and writing for percussion. Berg was always widely popular because of the constructivism. Messiaen was a presence there, especially his *Quartet for the End of Time* and his newest pieces such as *Quatre Études de rythme* (but not *Turangalîla*). Bartók was always somewhat acceptable, especially the style of his middle period, like the third and fourth string quartets (but not the fifth and sixth) the Second Piano Concerto (but not the third), as well as his use of folkloristic elements, which was considered interesting partly due to politics, because people thought it was free of the European tradition. Unfortunately, none of this added up to a coherent whole.

Every year, there were three or four orchestral concerts, and several new pieces were performed in them, including my *Fantasia for Orchestra*. There was a lot of chamber music, and works such as Alban Berg's *Vier Stücke*, op. 5 (*Four Pieces for Clarinet and Piano*), were very popular. And, of course, it was the beginning of awareness of Nono, Stockhausen, and Boulez.

I wasn't enthusiastic for this "Darmstadt" philosophy because of my father and my love of Schoenberg and Stravinsky. I was not one of those who chose one camp or the other; I admired them both. My interests were much wider and more general. I had a great admiration for Dallapiccola and some of the composers not acceptable to the ideologues, but I was also interested in the "new." How it affected my own work, I am not certain I can say. I was very young and at an early stage of my career. I have noticed that what I think consciously and what my ears cause me to write are two different things, and though they may be related, they are not identical.

By the time I got to Paris in 1955 and spent a lot of time with Boulez, the Darmstadt concept had become a sort of "inverted Palestrina." For instance, you could not write more than two conjunct notes from within a single octave—whatever the following note was, it had to be in a different octave. You had to avoid "reminiscence." You could analyze this in various ways, but in fact it became a stylistic mannerism, basically a negative thing, the avoidance of anything of which Boulez would have explained as the expectation of tonality that was not fulfilled. It was a "dislocation," and that's why Webern was so admired.

As I got to know Boulez more, musically and personally, I felt that at this time when he looked at music, for instance Debussy's *Jeux* or *Études*, it led him to the refinement of detail, quite regardless of the content of the music. In Debussy's étude that is a study in fourths, its many tempo changes inspired one of the Boulezean elements of the time: anything and everything can be permutated. Schoenberg had originated this idea in the *Harmonielehre*, where he permutated all available tonal chords, whether they are used in practice or not. The twelve-tone technique and serialism were seen as something different. People mixed them up quite freely then and now, but twelve-tone technique and serialism are technically two very different things.

Babbitt would define serialism as sequences of numbers producing many patterns, characterized by non-repeatability. The twelve-tone technique was formulated as a kind of general theory of motivic music, which was very much frowned upon by the Darmstadt adherents. The composers who wrote like that, Dallapiccola and myself included, would not have been acceptable at Darmstadt, where the important general stylistic technique was to transform dodecaphonic-inspired music by permutation.

For instance, on a trip to Italy I visited Bruno Maderna, who was writing a string quartet (which is a very good piece) that is in two movements. The first movement is a strict total permutation, the row is perpetually permutated according to magic square principles: a form of multiplication that leads to a perpetually ongoing reinvention of note patterns. In the first movement, the row is completely permutated each time it occurs so that it never recurs in its original form. It isn't motivic in any way. Nono would have learned this from Maderna, and they both would have gotten it from Hermann Scherchen.

The second movement was a free interpretation of the first movement. One of the influences for that was Messiaen's 1949 *Mode de valeurs d'intensités*, a key formulation of the permutational technique, though it is not exactly what Maderna did in his quartet. Messiaen invented a kind of mode that he composed freely with. It was misunderstood by the Darmstadt composers who thought it was a permutational technique, though it actually did not work like that. This led to Boulez's *Structures for Two Pianos, Book 1*, which was a total permutation piece where the unrepeatability of elements became *the* structural device. And that's what they saw in Webern too; and although it doesn't correspond to what Webern did, that is what they heard.

The influential part of this for me was that there was an element of "disguise" in these techniques, a negative thing. If you sat down and wrote a piece, with a twelve-tone row or freely, the second stage in making the composition was to disguise this by getting rid of things that stood out—i.e. to not concern oneself with a style of one's own, or a reflection of one's own invention, but to move towards a kind of canon of some sort, made from a pure language, and a progressive way of manipulating that language. It led to the movement that was briefly in favor known as "total serialism," led by Boulez and Henri Pousseur, and it was an influence on all the Darmstadt composers I have mentioned, as well as Messiaen.

The total serialism phase was short lived, and the key piece is of course Boulez's *Structures for Two Pianos*. I am not sure if Stockhausen composed any pieces like that, as his interests were broader, and his work was very much swayed by the fact that he worked in the Cologne electronic studio. Stockhausen was more of an experimenter. He used the same permutation techniques, but his work was very much affected by his electronic experience. The characteristic of Stockhausen as compared to Boulez is that he had a very imaginative sense of aural invention, more so than Boulez, who got stuck in what we called "Orientalism." *Le Marteau sans maître* was criticized at the time as being too geographic, or too Balinese, though, in fact, Boulez was a very widely cultured musician (so this should not be a surprise). Nono had all sorts of elements in his music of the time. If you take some of his early pieces, he may have started with a twelve-tone row, but you can't find it because of the permutations. There is no correlation between the durational and pitch-resultant content, and you cannot hear all those permutations anyway.

Like the Schoenberg School, one of the things that Boulez, Leibowitz, and the Darmstadt composers didn't like was decorative technique. In my *Fantasia*, which was not specifically written to be performed at Darmstadt, I freely decorate the row. As I mentioned before, it's called *Fantasia* because of Purcell, not because of the normal use of the title. I only have a vague recollection of composing it, but I remember it is a strict piece from the point of view of twelve-tone technique. The idea was that the long, measured durations were decorated by counterpoint in a slightly false medieval way. You can't just leave an E going in a slow tempo for fifteen seconds, it's boring. You have to do something with it. So you have the long note as a pedal, and then you elaborate it freely or decorate it with derived row forms.

I thought of my piece as an homage to Purcell in a way. The decorative technique led on for me, and it wasn't the last time I used it. Max Davies also influenced me with his research in Renaissance and medieval music, as well as his dissertation on Indian music, which was new to me at the time. The whole idea was to reintroduce structural decoration into music. My criticism of classical twelve-tone technique, which is related to what was thought in Darmstadt, is that it was one-dimensional.

We were also becoming interested in Heinrich Schenker at that time, who posited that tonal music had an underlying formal structure which was then elaborated on in the middle ground and foreground. We were trying to do that with our music. That was partly what Boulez was doing. If you look at his *Structures Book 2* or *Le Marteau sans maître*, you see a relationship between the formal row technique (such as he used it, and I don't think it was as good as something by, say, Babbitt) and the foreground which was done through the technique of his that I was most influenced by, which was his *bloc sonore* concept that he developed around that time. *Fantasia* was freer and more varied in its influences, and it had a more synthetic style, so it was not "Darmstadt" in that sense, but maybe Darmstadt wasn't really what we think of as "Darmstadt" either.

When I came back to England from Paris, everything was very different. At the time Messiaen kindly suggested that I stay another year in Paris and I might qualify for a First Prize, which is the top degree. As a foreigner, I got the Second Prize after one year, but getting any sort of prize or degree never impressed me as being of any serious interest whatsoever, and I lost the piece of paper soon thereafter anyway!

I was required to write a dissertation as part of Messiaen's class, which I had to read out in public. It was an analysis of the finale of Mozart's *Jupiter* Symphony, which I proposed was a synthesis of rondo and sonata forms. I did that mainly under the influence of the analysis by Simon Sechter that was published by Universal Edition. I read my paper before a board of examiners that passed it. Messiaen described it as a very personal approach, but I didn't think it was personal at all;

it was just stolen from Sechter! But Messiaen wouldn't have known that anyway because it would have been very different from his approach. The reason I mention it is that the piece that I wrote right after that, my String Quartet No.1, took the idea of the five or six themes of the *Jupiter* Symphony finale, which were combined with each other and also into a freer form, i.e., not Schoenberg, and not Webern, but some sort of synthesis between old and new.

Boulez was quite impressed by this 1957 quartet and tried very much to get it performed, but he didn't manage to find anyone to take on the badly written and complicated piece. Twenty years later I reworked it for the Arditti Quartet who said that it reminded them of Boulez's *Livre pour quatuor*, which they also played. When I rewrote it, I dedicated it to Boulez. I sent a letter to him and told him I was dedicating the piece to him because when I composed it I was very much under his influence (and superficially it looks like Boulez). He replied very quickly and said, "Ah, you are dedicating this piece to me and saying it was written when you were under my influence in order to tell me that you are no longer under my influence." I wrote an essay in response to his remark—"Letter to Pierre Boulez," published in my book *Finding the Key*—where I explained how I developed as a composer. Of course, what he was saying wasn't true, because I was and remain very much under his influence. Even now, when I write a kind of music which he certainly wouldn't have approved of or liked, I often find myself thinking, "I wonder what Pierre would have said about this."

My *Fantasia* was conducted at Darmstadt by Otto Matzerath, who was the chief conductor of the Frankfurt Radio Symphony Orchestra. It was done a few more times afterwards, most prominently by John Pritchard in Liverpool and by David Atherton sometime later on. I don't think it made any particular impression in Darmstadt, nor had any of my other pieces up to that point.

The first piece of mine that did make any impression on a slightly wider scale was *The Deluge, op. 7*, which was written immediately after the first string quartet. In between I had written a short piano piece, *Capriccio, op. 6*, again, based on the Mozart idea, but that was a deliberate answer (not that anyone would have appreciated it) to Stockhausen's *Klavierstück XI*. The characteristic of Stockhausen's John Cage-inspired piece is that it has little bits that can be played in any order. (It's printed on a single large sheet.) It was his first piece in which structure and chance operations were combined, and it was very influential. My *Capriccio* was written like the Stockhausen, using a lot of varied elements which were then combined in all possible ways. I wanted to show that by writing it the way I did, which is conventional in a sense, it would be like one of the versions of the Stockhausen. Any one version of *Klavierstück XI* would have been fixed merely by being played. Another performance would have been different, but still fixed, and I was showing the fixed nature of it with my piece.

I was friendly at that time with Cornelius Cardew, and he once told me that even when he did his Cage-inspired pieces, which on paper looked unformed and vague, he always wrote out a conventional version, which is the one he played. So my *Capriccio*, for what it's worth, was a piece whose parts could be played in any order, but I arranged an order for it because I thought that's what composers did!

There was a certain amount of interaction between Cage, Boulez and Stockhausen in the late 1950s. The third time I went to Darmstadt, in 1958, David Tudor was there and Cage was played. Around that time I went to a concert in Paris with Nono where some Cage was performed, and Nono observed that "if you listen to the sound of it, it doesn't sound all that different from other pieces being played at Darmstadt; it's the way it's done that is different."

I remember Boulez was sitting in a 1958 Darmstadt concert in which David Tudor played Cage and he was laughing like crazy, not taking it at all seriously, and I thought he was being rather scornful of it. Afterwards he said it was marvelous, but he actually laughed at it. However by then, what we think of as "Darmstadt" was over. Two things happened. Firstly Cage came, and secondly the Poles came, and this broadened and altered the perceptions of music. The Poles were Lutosławski, Penderecki, and Włodzimierz Kotoński. I didn't admire their style much, although I went to Warsaw and had a piece done there a year or two later, and I was quite friendly with them. Their music reminded me of "till ready music," their blocks of sound that were played randomly struck me as unserious and the music didn't interest me. I was much more interested in Schoenberg, followed by Messiaen, Boulez, and Webern.

## 6. HANNS EISLER

*JVZ: Before I went to study with Goehr in Cambridge, Hanns Eisler was a name familiar to me, but I didn't know much about him other than he was a student of Schoenberg's, worked closely with Bertolt Brecht, and had written some scores for American films. It took me a while to learn about him and his works, but it was thanks to Goehr's connection to him and his advising me to listen to certain Eisler works over the years that I came to have a great appreciation of his music.*

*There is no doubt about the fact that Eisler is sadly neglected and underperformed nowadays, though his songs, especially those from his* Hollywood Songbook, *do get performances now and then in Los Angeles and elsewhere. His* German Symphony *(which Goehr attended the premiere of, conducted by his father Walter in West Berlin in 1958) is a great work and should get more attention, along with his many excellent chamber and orchestral works. One of the important lessons I have learned from my own study of Eisler is that a composer can utilize the latest "radical" methods in a way that can be made into music which has a more traditional effect and is, perhaps, more readily performable and "audience friendly."*

*It was a lucky break for Goehr to have Eisler as a mentor. Of course the friendship between Goehr's father, Walter, and his fellow Schoenberg pupil allowed for the introduction, as this chapter details. It is quite obvious that Eisler took a liking to the young Goehr, for various reasons that become apparent in Goehr's recollections of him, and the relationship was very important to Goehr at just the right moment in his career. Significantly, too, both men held political beliefs of the left which helped to bond them.*

*I feel that Goehr's music evolved in a very different way because of his mentor than it would have otherwise. Of course Goehr's early song cycles* Warngedichte *and* In Theresienstadt, *his* Tryptich *of music theater pieces* (Sonata about Jerusalem, Shadow Play *and*

Naboth's Vineyard), *and his first opera,* Arden Must Die, *all exhibit Eisler's influence. This influence has continued with several other works throughout Goehr's lifetime, such as* The Death of Moses *from 1993, and his 2010 opera* Promised End, *based on Shakespeare's* King Lear.

*I find Eisler to be a fascinating figure. From my perspective as an American, I am sad about Eisler's deportation from the USA in 1948 during the time of the House Un-American Activities Committee (HUAC) and Senator Joseph McCarthy's anti-communist purges, which ruined so many lives. His time in Hollywood coincided with the period when German and Austrian immigrant composers—many of them students of Schoenberg, then living in Los Angeles—constituted the group of the most important film composers of the era. Eisler was a very successful film composer and probably would have stayed at it had he not been sent back to Austria and then East Germany by force.*

*Composers who were mentored by Eisler are a rarity, so it was a very lucky experience for Goehr, and his account of his relationship with Eisler provides a unique glimpse of the older composer, and one that is of great interest historically. I began our conversation by asking Goehr when he first knew of Eisler and how he came to meet him.*

AG: I was aware of Hanns Eisler at a young age, knowing that he was a friend of my father's. I met him in 1956 in Paris right after Bertolt Brecht died. I went there with my father where we saw performances of Brecht's *Galileo* and *Mother Courage*. At the same time, the Berlin Ensemble was in Paris, and my father took me to see Eisler who was there with them.

It wasn't an altogether happy visit. Eisler was writing music for a film in a little hotel room with a piano. He was reasonably nice at first, but he looked at my *Fantasia for Orchestra* that was about to be performed at Darmstadt, and on the first page spotted three successive chromatic notes

*Hanns Eisler in Hollywood, 1943. Courtesy of Eisler-Haus Leipzig*

in the cello part and said, "One doesn't write for the cello like that." It seemed a rather stupid criticism to me, and he never turned the page but kept on about the chromatic notes. Then the conversation moved on, and Boulez came up and I told Eisler about the new *Le Marteau sans maître*, which he dismissed as "reactionary", and said it was of no interest to him. He was quite abrasive and horrible, and I was pleased when my father and I finally got out of the room.

My father sent me back to the hotel that evening to deliver a score to Eisler, and I was going to leave it at the desk, but they phoned up and he told them to send me up to his room. By this time he had started on a bottle of whisky (which he liked very much) and he was very friendly. He asked about Boulez and *Le Marteau* and wondered where he could get a score, etc. He was quite different and I liked him much better than I had earlier in the day.

I didn't meet him again until 1959 when I went to East Berlin with my father, who conducted the premiere of Eisler's *German Symphony*. A few years later, I was working at the BBC producing concerts and I arranged for the performances of several of Eisler's pieces, including the *German Symphony*, and Eisler came to London for them. I showed him more of my scores and he was much more sympathetic than he had been in Paris. He gave me good advice, and I saw him a few more times before he died.

The reason why I got interested in Eisler is much harder to describe, but it was partly because of politics, and partly out of my reaction to what was going on in Darmstadt. Many composers, not only those on the left, were interested in the USSR Communist Party Central Committee's tribunal in which Shostakovich and Prokofiev were criticized. Britten and Copland both made statements in support of the Russian composers saying that music should become more "audience friendly." I was intrigued by that, and I was interested in Eisler because he was the only one of Schoenberg's pupils who, after his first few works, attempted to modify the twelve-tone technique to fit into a more political vision of music that would "speak" to people.

Eisler's political music primarily took the form of songs, and, along with Britten and Copland, he was one of the best song composers of the mid-twentieth century. There are perhaps 200 to 300 Eisler songs, some of them à la carte political songs; others, like *Hollywood Elegies*, are more sophisticated, and are obviously the ones I like best.

Eisler was a very fluent composer—he could write very well and very easily—and he was good at exactly the thing that most of the Schoenberg students were not good at: the scherzo form. He was very good at writing fast music, and you can hear this in his *Fourteen Ways of Describing Rain*, which is a collection of fourteen scherzos, all different from each other. No one else in the Schoenberg world could do anything like that.

Eisler told me an anecdote that relates to this. He was at one time living in Schoenberg's house in Vienna because he was very poor and Schoenberg took him in. They composed separately in the mornings and would meet at lunchtime. Over one such lunch Schoenberg asked him, "How many bars did you write this morning?" Eisler said, "Oh about 120 or so," Schoenberg's face fell, and Eisler asked, "How many did you write?" To which Schoenberg replied, "Only about eight." Then Schoenberg said, "What was the meter of your 120 bars?" Eisler said, "3/8." "Ah," said Schoenberg, "mine were 12/8 in a very slow tempo!"

Schoenberg had a very high opinion of Eisler (although he didn't like the politics much), and he thought Eisler was a very gifted composer, which indeed he was. After Berg and Webern, Eisler ranks high among the next one or two of Schoenberg's pupils. He may not have been quite in the class of Webern and Berg, but he was pretty good!

Something that intrigued me about him when I got to know him better was that he had a reputation as a very devoted communist, but in fact, as much as Karl Marx played a part in his thinking, he was a very educated man, about the most educated composer I have ever known, and he was very well read and knew literature and philosophy, etc. François Villon sometimes seemed as important to him as Marx. He suffered a great deal for his politics. He did very well in America and his best pieces were in the 1930s and 40s, but after he was deported from the US in 1948 and went back to East Berlin, he wasn't altogether happy and he didn't compose much between then and his death in 1963—there are hardly any pieces from that time.

Most of his American pieces—nonets, septets, and chamber symphonies—contained music he had written for films, and his pieces of that time, with a few exceptions, are a bit fragmentary, which I think marred them. Some of them had a quality of their own, and sometimes they were just very good counterpoint.

Apart from the obvious influence of my *Little Symphony, op. 15* taking its title from Eisler's *Kleine Sinfonie*, as well as the idea of the variations in the first movement, I was very much attracted to his personality, and appreciated how he looked at my pieces and gave me good advice. I don't think his music influenced me to any great extent, although, certainly, sometimes I tried to imitate something he had done. I suppose he represented something in the Schoenbergian world that attracted me. Perhaps it was his quasi-tonal use of twelve-tone material—he arranged his rows in a way that provided tonal relationships—which was similar to what I did, though I didn't do it the same way.

The *German Symphony* is a very striking work and has in it the best piece of pure music he ever wrote, namely the Allegro finale. He compared it to Beethoven's Ninth Symphony, which became a vocal piece in its last movement, but Eisler's is vocal all the way through. It is known as the *Deutsche Sinfonie*, but he originally called it the *Deutsches Miserere*, and the last movement is a sort of collapse, the opposite of the hope of Beethoven's Ninth. That Allegro shows what a good composer he was. It is a long piece, perhaps ten minutes long, and it really is beautifully written.

It wasn't a question of trying to create "audience friendly" music that, in Eisler's terms, would have attracted the proletariat. In fact, the proletariat wasn't attracted to the music of Eisler or anyone else. It might have been an aim in East Germany, where he was the national composer, and the government made a point of promoting it, but they ignored his more abstract pieces, which were not played at all. He was a very good teacher and had a number of pupils in East Germany, including the English composer David Blake, who went there to study with him.

I would meet Eisler in his home in East Berlin when I was there, or in London when he came to visit. We talked a lot about poetry and philosophy, and he was very inspiring, as well as being a very good critic. When I gave him a piece to look at, he would have a good comment. I remember showing him my *Suite, op. 11*, which I wrote for the Aldeburgh Festival. He told me that it was very good and that he liked what he saw, but also said that you only become a real composer when you try all the different forms of music making; otherwise your work descends into genre music. The criticism he implied is that I had to work more objectively to fill big forms. And my pieces for flute and piano and my violin concerto from this time certainly show an attempt at doing what he suggested.

As I mentioned before, I went to East Berlin with my father when he conducted the premiere of Eisler's *German Symphony* on April 24, 1959 at the Berlin State Opera. The work had mostly been written in the 1930s and 40s, but wasn't finished until 1957. The premiere was a very striking occasion. There was a very large choir and excellent soloists, including the soprano Irmgard Arnold who was a very good singer. The audience wasn't big—he had no popular following—and what there was of it consisted of the East Berlin elite. I remember being very moved by it, especially the Allegro which I already mentioned. The first part of the symphony is a setting of Brecht and Eisler texts for four voices and orchestra, and one or two of them are quite tragic in feeling. The last poem is from a little book published by Brecht called *Kriegsfibel*, where it is illustrated by a photograph of defeated German soldiers. There is also a setting of a Brecht poem (that Kurt Weill also did marvelously) about veterans of the First World War marching through Potsdam, called *Zu Potsdam unter den Eichen*.

When the *German Symphony* was performed in London, there was an English baritone who was singing in the performance, and I remember he was putting all the expression he could into it, trying to represent all the suffering of the poem with a very upfront opera-type *espressivo*. Eisler, who was a very small man with one functioning tooth, walked up to the baritone, who was a very large man, grinned at him and said, "Look, don't sing it like that. Sing it like Schubert. The words are grim enough for the poem to speak by itself and it will speak better if you sing it in a much more restrained, Schubertian manner." That struck me as an example of the kind of Brechtian/Eislerian alienation technique where you make something more expressive not by actually singing it full throttle, but by holding back. That is just one story that showed me something about what he thought about the role of music, especially vocal music, and the whole concept of restraint is something that caught on with me.

Although he defended Schoenberg at all times, even in East Germany where Schoenberg was under attack, he felt, like many Schoenberg pupils, there weren't two Schoenbergs in the world; there was only one, and you couldn't emulate him, and Eisler didn't. Many years ago when a film was being made about Eisler, I said, to the great annoyance of everybody, that if you said that Arnold Schoenberg was a quasi-Beethoven figure, then Eisler would be a kind of Mendelssohn figure, because he mastered the lighter forms of music: scherzos, etc.

Also very characteristic of Eisler, and something that influenced me greatly, were his conclusions and endings. The songs always end in very strange ways, something also characteristic of Schoenberg. They are not always the obvious cadential endings at all; they just stop, or they go somewhere else. That very much appealed to me, and many times I felt myself doing that and thinking about Eisler. Many great song composers, Benjamin Britten included, set the poem and when the words come to an end, so does the song. It's all about the words. Eisler was a very good song composer, and the best of his songs are really magnificent.

Eisler was a very good choral composer too. I got the John Alldis Choir to perform *Gegen den Krieg, op. 55*, "Against the War," which is a beautiful set of chorale variations à la Bach. One of my major influences from Eisler is that he introduced me to the idea of the chorale prelude, which has figured right through my work since. It might have originally come from Schoenberg to some extent, but it comes to me more specifically from Eisler. (You don't find it in Webern or Berg, but you find it here and there in Schoenberg, like in the *Suite, op. 29*.) The popular song in Eisler's hands is treated very much like a chorale prelude. He very consciously thought that the chorale prelude was a way of combining and synthesizing different styles of music, so that you could, say, have a popular song and treat it polyphonically, just as in the way Bach treated very simple Lutheran chorales and then elaborated them into very great pieces.

Eisler's last proposed piece, which he never managed to write, was going to be a symphony modeled on Mendelssohn's *Reformation* Symphony, which is a setting of Lutheran chorales made into a symphony. Eisler was going to use popular songs, perhaps communist ones, in a popular style. The commission was from the Gewandhausorchester in Leipzig, where Mendelssohn lived and was a conductor. He talked a lot about it to me but he never actually wrote any of it. He was at the end of his life, though he was only in his mid-60s, and I think his inspiration had left him, partly due to many disappointments.

He had proposed writing an opera on Faust—a communist version—of which he published the libretto. He was inspired by Thomas Mann's book about writing his novel *Doctor Faustus* (*The Story of a Novel: The Genesis of Doctor Faustus*). He put more into that project than almost anything else he had ever done, and he really wanted to write this opera, but the Communist Party stopped him because in the second act, Faust betrayed the revolution. The second act takes place in Atlantis, which is obviously the USA. Faust is there with a lovely girl and everything is nice, and then he goes back to this ruined country, obviously Germany, where everything is destroyed. Faust sings something like "My God, who in their right mind would come back to this." This offended the East German government very much and they forbade him to compose it. It broke his heart. (Incidentally, after Eisler's death, his widow Steffi suggested that I compose the opera with his libretto, which is wonderful, but I thought it belonged to its time and to somebody else and I wouldn't be able to do it.)

All of this was quite influential on my first opera, *Arden Must Die*. It's a Brechtian piece in its conception and production, and the music has some Eislerian elements in it. (However, the most important influence in my opera was, in fact, Charles Ives, because of the rhythmic technique I used. *Arden Must Die* is full of lies, and whenever anybody told a lie, I moved the natural emphasis from a strong beat on to a weak beat, which caused some difficulty in performance.)

In a way, Eisler was very paternal towards me. He suggested many things I should read and music I should listen to, and I always followed his advice. He was certainly a mentor to me in the kind of pieces I chose to write (sometimes successfully, sometimes not), and his inspiration goes right through my life. My opera *Behold the Sun* has a lot of Eisler's influence in it (and it's also quasi-Handelian). The idea I subscribe to of not illustrating the text (i.e., *no* word painting), but treating the music as a kind of commentary to the text, all that comes from the Brecht-Eisler world.

In terms of the chorale prelude, I have used Gregorian chants often as models for something that could be the "chorale" subject of a chorale prelude, like in my ... *a musical offering (JSB 1985)..., op. 46*. Earlier on, going right back to the beginning of my work, back to Manchester and Max Davies, I don't know whether my *Fantasia, op. 4*, or Max Davies's *Alma Redemptoris Mater* was first (it doesn't matter), but what both our pieces had in common was that they treated the material—in my case a dodecaphonic row—like a chorale prelude, measuring it into longer lengths of notes like quasi-rhythmic serialism, and arranging a slow structure, either in one or two parts, and then ornamenting it. Of course, "ornamentation" was a dirty word in the Schoenberg school, but I did it and Max Davies did too in his *Alma Redemptoris Mater*, which is also a massive elaboration of a chant. Of course that way of composing is much more characteristic of early and middle period Maxwell Davies than it is of me. I didn't stick with that direction, but the first movement of my Violin Concerto, op. 13 from that time, which I had shown to Eisler, is a chorale prelude. All my life since then I have liked chorale preludes. (I proposed them as an alternative to fugue when I was Professor of Music at Cambridge: students could write a fugue or a chorale prelude as part of their composition Tripos exam. It was offered as an alternative for many years, but I don't think a single student ever did it, which is a shame.) The use of chorale prelude is definitely the most important thing I learned from Eisler, and I still think it has limitless possibilities for a composer, because it is an excellent way of connecting and synthesizing different elements into a single work. I still use the concept—not in a black-and-white sense, but when I plan what I might do in a piece, it's often part of the plan.

Before my father died, he wanted to do an orchestration of some of Bach's chorale preludes. That's because he didn't like the organ and he thought those magnificent pieces would be better served by a modern orchestra. (This is clearly out of date as a concept these days.) When he died in 1960, I thought the best way I could remember him was by writing a set of chorale preludes. Bach's *Clavier-Übung* starts with a *St. Anne Prelude* and ends with a *St. Anne Fugue*, and in between are twelve chorale preludes. I thought to write something like that but I never managed it. At that time I wrote about fifty bars of a piece like it and abandoned it, and instead, I wrote the *Little Symphony, op. 15*, in memory of my father.

Eisler was very ironic and humorous, but underneath that there was deep feeling—including feeling for literature, and feeling for music. He told me that his father was a philosopher, his mother was a German "market woman" from Leipzig, he was half Jewish, and they moved to Vienna when Eisler was very young. I don't know the whole truth of his life as he was a bit of an exaggerator, but it might all be true.

In terms of his politics, I think that in common with all of us, the reality of East European communism was not what he wanted or dreamed of. He saw the faults of it, and the things that he didn't like and spoke about brought him trouble. He would have run into bigger trouble if he hadn't been of a family which was well established as part of the East German Communist aristocracy (his brother was a government minister). He got himself out of difficulty by use of the concept of stupidity which he wrote a lot about. He authored a book about stupidity in music. He thought that music was supposed to make people more discriminating and more intelligent, but a lot of music had the opposite effect, making people more stupid. Politically, he thought that many of the mistakes that disillusioned him about the state in which he lived were due to stupidity. I thought his view was too simple, and that he attributed too much to stupidity instead of malevolence and corruption.

It's partly an adoption of Schoenbergian thinking on music that repetition, ornamentation, and rodomontade of one kind or another ought to be cut out of music. Eisler tried, in that sense, to create a Schoenbergian philosophy which would fit in with communist philosophy, which is clearly an impossible task. The concept of using music for political purposes has been outdated since the advent of pop music. When Eisler was alive, there was light music with dreadful texts that could do this, but the development of pop music cancels all this out. Political statements are made by pop musicians, not by serious composers whose attempts to do so don't reach anybody. It's impossible to do and it doesn't have any impact. Dealing with contemporary events in art is as good as futile because things change too quickly.

My own political pieces, such as my opera *Behold the Sun*, comment by taking an historical subject that has clear relevance. From that point of view, *Behold the Sun* anticipated religious fundamentalism. I chose the subject because the Anabaptists stood for communists in literature. In fact it anticipated Christian and later Muslim fundamentalism, and terrorism. Regrettably the opera has never been performed properly, but from my point of view that's what it was all about.

## 7. ALAN HACKER

*JVZ: One of the best things to happen to composers is when we form a close professional connection with a performer that takes our music to an unexpected place. It's a two-way street where, in working closely with a player, you are able to write a piece that fits their talents like a glove, with the result that both composer and performer equally benefit more than usual. One of the ways this works is when a performer is able to take what the composer writes specifically for them and "feels" their way through the music in a way that adds something beyond what the composer imagined. This kind of connection doesn't happen every day, but when it does, it's a very gratifying experience for both; a sum greater than the parts.*

*Goehr has had important relationships with great performers throughout his career. These resulted in major works, such as the* Romanza for Cello and Orchestra, op. 24, *for Jacqueline du Pré, the Piano Concerto, op. 32, for Daniel Barenboim, and Piano Quintet, op. 69, and other pieces for pianist Peter Serkin. However, those were more coincidental professional working relationships, whereas his relationship with the British clarinetist Alan Hacker (1938–2012) over the period of a few years in the 1960s and 1970s holds a special place in Goehr's thinking, as he learned so much from it that has influenced his work ever since. Because of that, we felt that Hacker had to have a place in this book among Goehr's teachers, mentors, and wider influences.*

AG: I started thinking about Alan Hacker's role in my life as a composer by remembering something he said in jest about a piece of mine I had written for him that "it might be said that I wrote it myself."

I first met Alan in the early 1960s when Harry Birtwistle brought him to see me. The two of them had been co-students of Reginald Kell at the Royal Academy of Music. Alan would

*Alan Hacker. Photo by Laelia Goehr*

go on to have a great influence on me, as he did on Harry, and on Max Davies. He was remarkable in many ways, with wide interests which extended much further than the clarinet. It might be said that he was a composer who didn't compose!

In the late 1960s Alan was the mainstay in our Music Theatre Ensemble, to which he brought some of the extraordinary players that we had. After I went to America, he joined Birtwistle's Pierrot Players, and later Max Davies's Fires of London.

A significant development in Alan's career was when he managed to get hold of the mouthpiece of Charles Draper, who was an eminent clarinetist in London from the 1890s through the first half of the twentieth century. Alan discovered that Draper's mouthpiece produced a very different sound from what was a normal clarinet sound at that time. Alan was then the second clarinet in the London Philharmonic, and I understand that he was asked to leave the orchestra because his sound didn't fit in with the other players in the wind section. As far as I can remember from what I heard and what he told me, the sound the mouthpiece produced was much more like a trumpet. He said that the sound that clarinetists were making at that time in the classics was, in fact, what Brahms called "echotone," and the real sound was much bolder.

At the same time, he was interested in the re-creation of the basset clarinet which could play notes down to a sixth lower that a modern A or B-flat clarinet. Mozart's Clarinet Concerto for Anton Stadler was written for the basset clarinet and uses those lower notes. When we hear the concerto played on a modern clarinet, it is, in fact, an adaptation with those lower notes transposed. Alan was very keen to restore the original sound of Mozart's concerto and clarinet quintet by performing them on the basset clarinet as intended.

Players didn't fully know the instrument, he believed. Echotone was only one of many tones available on the clarinet. To know the instrument meant being able to produce a variety of tone colors, but also to access the higher range, which required a system of alternative fingerings that yielded slightly different colors. For instance, he could play a trill with the two notes in it being the identical or very near the same pitch levels, but created with different fingerings with different sonic results.

I became fascinated by his unique approach to his instrument. This was a time when there was quite a lot of experimentation on wind instruments. For instance, overblowing an instrument to create a chord-like sound ("multiphonics") was discussed in the book *New Sounds for Woodwind*, by the Italian composer Bruno Bartolozzi, published in the 1960s. Wind players, certainly the ones interested in performing modern music, were enthusiastic about such extensions to sound on their instruments. Alan, however, was conspicuously hostile to these developments; he felt the experimenting with the instrument without a compositional purpose was pointless. (However, he did experiment with creating fingerings for multiphonic sounds and found that many of them were different from those in the Bartolozzi book.)

Alan had a considerable effect on my way of writing for wind instruments. I wrote some pieces especially for him, including the first of my triptych of music theater pieces, *Naboth's Vineyard, op. 25*, which has some extended clarinet cadenzas for him. That part is what gave rise to his jest quoted above. He didn't actually write anything, but he did transform what I had written much further than I would have been able to. In the second of my music theater triptych, *Shadowplay, op. 30*, I wrote an alto sax part for Alan which used similar methods to his clarinet techniques, but I don't think after that he did any more extended work for the saxophone. I also wrote my most special piece for him, a solo work, *Paraphrase on the Dramatic Madrigal "Il Combattimento di Tancredi e Clorinda" by Cl. Monteverdi, op. 28*, which combined some of Monteverdi's motifs with a virtuoso technique I had learned from him. The piece was performed onstage among the props from the dramatic work. His recording of the piece shows the variety of sounds and techniques that he was able to bring to it. It was much more than a normal performance; it was a creative contribution.

It's worth remembering that at that time of so-called "total serialism" which began with Messiaen's *Mode de valeurs et d'intensités*, the idea was to submit the various dynamic levels—*pp, p mp, mf, f ff,* etc.—to individual units that could be manipulated according to a serial practice. A good example apart from Messiaen's piece—and well before its time—is the second movement of Webern's *Variations for Piano, op. 27*.

It is a kind of scherzo in which each group, section of chords or single notes (generally a two-part structure) has a specific dynamic level. Babbitt believed that ideally such techniques would be best realized by electronic music where, to some extent, the individual intensities, dynamic ranges, and sound qualities could be controlled exactly, in a way that was hardly possible in human performance.

Alan and I were briefly able to realize a unique relationship between composer and performer, and it certainly influenced my way of thinking right up to the present. It's difficult to demonstrate the ways composers and performers interact when they are not the same person, like Paganini. But I'd like to mention the violinist Samuel Dushkin's partnership with Stravinsky, who wrote his Violin Concerto for him. Dushkin's original way of playing the violin greatly influenced Stravinsky's composition of the work, and is directly present in the concerto from the very first chord. Similarly, you can hear Alan's influence on the pieces I wrote for him, as well as in the way I have composed for wind instruments since.

## 8. SCHOENBERG

*JVZ: The music and theoretical writings of Arnold Schoenberg have loomed large in Goehr's life as they did for many of his generation, just as they had for his father's and indeed my own. In many ways Schoenberg remains a seminal figure for all composers, whether it is on a conscious level or not. I realize there are both positive and negative connotations to that, as many composers are famous for asserting a rejection of Schoenberg in crafting their work, but by creating music as a reaction to it, these composers are coming to terms with it just like those who view Schoenberg more favorably as an influence. Whatever you might think of it all now, there is no doubt that Schoenberg is a giant of our art who changed the course of music forever. He is inescapable.*

*I became a composer because of Schoenberg's music, which I first encountered by chance at the age of eighteen via a recording of his Violin Concerto. I did not then know that such music existed and I was so taken with the sound world that I vowed then and there to learn how to make such music myself. Apart from providing the starting point of my lifelong quest, Schoenberg has been the single most important source of musical ideas and practice in my life. At the time that I was about to go off to study with Goehr in Cambridge, his connection to Schoenberg through his father, but also through his idiosyncratic compositional technique of the time, was a huge selling point for me. I was also thrilled to learn of Goehr's 1970s TV series on Schoenberg's life and works that had been made by the BBC (and which is still available for viewing on YouTube).*

*Much of my early study with Goehr included lots of questions concerning the work of Schoenberg (as well as Webern and Berg) and how I could utilize the lessons from it for my own purposes. I did have an obsession for it (and still do to a certain extent), and the fact that the same could be said of Goehr only intensified my* interest, though he would have been the first person to tell me not to rely on it too much. But for me, to have a teacher who shared my deep love of Schoenberg's music was the best thing I could think of.

Consequently, Goehr and I have discussed Schoenberg's works frequently over the years. His insights into the music and theories via his father and his own studies have been invaluable to me. These are not typical insights into the work, such as counting notes or analyzing classical Mozartian phrase structure, but something deeper and much more interesting, like getting to the essence of the actual sound of it. This involved exploring the brilliant compositional and philosophical strategies that Schoenberg employed in creating it. My lifetime quest to understand Schoenberg is a gift that just keeps on giving, and I feel very lucky to have been able to plumb those depths with my teacher.

In addition, I am a proponent of Schoenberg's theoretical writings. While Style and Idea *was huge for me, I also find value in the controversial books on harmony, composition, and counterpoint, in that they approach the subjects from the point of view of a composer. They aren't perfect as textbooks, but they certainly work as an impetus to actually write notes on paper and move them around, to find the best solutions to harmonic and contrapuntal sequences. I find them to be very good sources of ideas for my own teaching of these subjects, which are vital in the training of young composers.*

Of course, Goehr's views on everything I brought up are not always in complete accord with my own, but these points of difference have provided fodder for very interesting discussions over the years that have taught me a great deal, and some of these are part of the discussion that we record here. Goehr had a good idea of what he wanted to say about Schoenberg for this book, which I supplemented with various aspects of the music and educational writings of Schoenberg that I wanted to be part of it, too. His well thought out responses to these are especially important from the point of view of his looking back on the evolution of his thoughts on

*Arnold Schoenberg, Berlin class, with Walter Goehr over his left shoulder. Goehr Archive*

*the subject over many decades. It is important for young composers to take note that whatever they think of their influences today, this will gradually change throughout their lifetimes, but this constantly continuing process will enrich their understanding of the art as they get older and more experienced.*

AG: Schoenberg was always there in the background when I was growing up, especially in my relationship to my father, but it didn't really affect me then. In many ways, my father reflected a Schoenbergian attitude, and he had the highest possible regard for Schoenberg. I can't remember the first time I heard his music and I didn't know any of it until I was sixteen or seventeen. I remember going to a performance my father conducted of the Piano Concerto with Peter Stadlen. Hardly any of Schoenberg's music was ever programmed in Britain before the 1950s, and the only conductor performing it was my father. Additionally, there weren't any records of his music available then, except maybe *Verklärte Nacht*.

I'm not sure how I first became interested in Schoenberg as a composer. Probably it was a case of the apple falling not far from the tree. It wasn't until I got to Manchester that I took a serious interest in the theory of his work through Richard Hall. I didn't know any of the music but I had heard about the twelve-tone technique. Hall had no particular affection for Schoenberg as a composer; it wasn't his kind of thing. But because Hall was interested in numerology, he was attracted to the idea of the twelve-tone row, which he had learned about from his Manchester friends Charlotte Demant, the former wife of Hanns Eisler, and her partner, Arnold Rosé, the violinist of the Rosé Quartet. I think at Manchester I had looked at Schoenberg's piano music, specifically the *Six Little Pieces, op. 19*, and the *Three Pieces, op. 11*, and would have been able to play some of them, but not the third movement of Op. 11, which is intolerably difficult!

I had a conversation with Oliver Knussen a few years ago that started with an article in *The New York Review of Books* about an exhibition in Paris of paintings by Giacometti, Balthus, and another French painter. The thesis of the exhibition was that there these artists were united by an alternative type of modernism. They didn't follow the modernism of expressionism or cubism, but instead, through representational art, they created an alternative modernism that was not the same as the old modernism, nor was it particularly traditional. The writer described it as a new way of looking at representations of nature, and explained that here was a "distancing" going on. It was an interesting and convincing article, and it made me think of Schoenberg.

For Boulez and his followers, Schoenberg's music of interest ended with *Jakobsleiter*. They (as I do) admired the early works like the First Chamber Symphony, the *Five Pieces for Orchestra*, and *Erwartung*, etc.—the works of the period up to the First World War, more or less. Boulez thought the methodology of the twelve-tone works was interesting, but he didn't really like the music much. He performed it because he was a "paid-up Schoenbergian," but he didn't actually enjoy the sound of it. It's generally true to say that whereas people can accept the first part of Schoenberg's output, the subsequent part, which is called "classical twelve-tone", has a harder time and is not accepted in the same way as his earlier work, and possibly never will be.

Although there was and is a preference for the sound of the music from the first half of Schoenberg's life, the music of the second half was probably more important, as he was embarking on what one might describe as an impossible task to recreate the musical language. He was very keen not to overstate the methodological aspect of his work: it was twelve-tone *music* not *twelve-tone* music. Whatever one thinks of those pieces—and I love some of them, like the last two string quartets, the *Suite*, the *Variations for Orchestra*, and others of the later pieces—whether I like them or not is of relative unimportance; the important thing is to assess what role they play in musical thinking in their own time and after Schoenberg's death, up to now.

One thing I very clearly remember, is that when I wrote, together with my father, the article "Schoenberg's Way to the Twelve-tone Technique," the hero of it was *Erwartung*. Certainly in my early twenties, my ideal life would have been to rewrite *Erwartung*. That's the musical language I admired. It took me a little while to realize that not only could I not do it, but that no one could create a composition with that kind of freedom of technical application—hardly any repetition, no sequences, nothing very formal, and with a very free harmonic language. We tried to speculate how that came about—through the use of single notes, etc.—but the important thing for me was that it was a heroic thing to do.

In fact, what interests me most in music is synthesis. Now to some extent, the twelve-tone technique was a very harsh way of rescuing the music of the past (as Schoenberg believed he was doing), and to make it relevant. The real synthesis occurs in the later pieces after about op. 30—on the one hand with the *Ode to Napoleon*, on the other hand with *Kol Nidre* and the Second Chamber Symphony. I concluded my conversation about this with Oliver Knussen by throwing a brick in the water, proposing that had Schoenberg lived twenty-five or even just ten years longer, he would have come up with a new form of composition that, in purely technical terms, would have been described as synthesis—something between tonal practice and dodecaphonic motivic practice. Later I realized that the weak spot of my remark is that you cannot separate these elements from his composition. You can't say, this is twelve-tone composition, this is atonal composition, and this is synthesized composition, because in fact, it's all muddled up. You are just saying, "It's Schoenberg."

I have two further points to make from this discussion. One is historic: that the direction Schoenberg seemed to be going in when he died is diametrically opposed to what was happening everywhere else. While others were going towards a "purity of system," Schoenberg was moving in the opposite direction, creating a synthesis of different elements. (Stravinsky was first moving towards synthesis in the *Canticum Sacrum*, but then changed directions towards a Webern-like purity of system.) Knussen said that a key example of this was the Second Chamber Symphony, originally written after the first one and then abandoned. If you listen to it, the first two movements—which were written in 1913 and aren't quite as good as the First Chamber Symphony—are slightly vaguer in intention, but nevertheless resemble a lot of the whole tone and Schoenbergian harmony you find in his work of that time. But the final third slow movement, which was composed many years later when he decided to try and save this piece, is written in a different style from the first two movements, and I suspect that from the difference in characteristics between the last movement and the earlier two—as he wrote in an article "One always Returns"—he wasn't going back, but instead was going forward to something else. And while the later final movement is clearly related motivically to the earlier movements, the last is a slow piece and the pattern is slow–fast–slow, with the best piece being the middle scherzo, which is very good. We then discussed the other pieces which enter into this. The best piece by far is *Kol Nidre*, which in compositional technique is not that dissimilar from Bartók's dealing with traditional music. It is a sort of serial music done with motivic modal/tonal means.

The opposite piece is the *Ode to Napoleon* which is very much a "row" piece, but with repeated elements which end up being tonal or quasi-tonal. Knussen suggested to me that the *Suite* for septet, which is a very formal twelve-tone piece, also has elements of harmony and repetitive incantations or patterns of some kind which keep recurring, and that this is the same technique as in *Ode to Napoleon*. He wanted to say that the incipient nature of a "mutant" tonalism, if we can call it that, is already in the nature of the twelve-tone technique, but this one is not free, it's hard-edged and it has corners. (Stravinsky said about it that he thought it was like Max Reger, but it's nothing like Reger; it is a thing of its own.) It has a touch of academicism about it, it's very rigid, and when you look at the other pieces of the time, which admittedly he wrote because he needed money, such as the *Theme and Variations for band, op. 43a*, or the *Theme and Variations on a Recitative for Organ, op. 40*, these pieces are consciously formal, and they are not as good as the *Kol Nidre*. All these different elements and contrasts within half a dozen pieces at the most suggest that "in the dark", Schoenberg was working towards something that he was approaching in a number of different ways, but that he possibly didn't get final results. It was very late in his life and at the same time he was writing the String Trio, op. 45 and the *Phantasy for Violin with Piano Accompaniment, op. 47,* which are clearly expressionistic works. So it's rather a complicated relationship.

Of course, talking about Schoenberg's work using this type of synthesis is my own personal way of thinking about it, and so I am really talking about myself. I thought that, systematically, within the construction of twelve-tone rows there are tonal considerations. There are examples of where Schoenberg altered tone rows and changed notes around in order to later create a tonal relationship in a piece. That is probably the link in all these elements. When Schoenberg is writing "tonal," rather stiff music, he is still himself, and he is doing what one might have criticized him for earlier—being too literal, which he got away from, but then comes back to. (There is a practical aspect to this as a way of working, of course; changing things around because he liked the sound of something better than the way it was.)

In a discussion I had about this with Milton Babbitt, he criticized the First Chamber Symphony because the imitation of the motives is literal, and he disliked that. Literalism is built into the twelve-tone technique as Schoenberg used it, because he thought it to be a general system, of which the most important element was the motive.

We have all tried to get away from that literalism—Webern for instance—but Schoenberg persists in being a very literal composer with the tonal pieces that come near the end of his life. For instance, the main *Kol Nidre* motive is an imitation of one which he developed from an old setting of the text that a rabbi had given him. He derives further motives from that one, and once he has established them in the piece, he sticks to them extremely in a way that I suppose I have spent my life trying to get away from. My attitude towards the whole system of dodecaphony after my first six or so pieces was to move away from literalism because I took what Babbitt thought very much to heart. One *can* admire the literalism of Schoenberg as a sort of exact drawing that is wrongly placed. There are many who think that these late tonal pieces of his are dreadful—Stravinsky did— but they have a sound world of their own because of Schoenberg's distinct characteristics. At the very least, I think this is a very interesting aspect of Schoenberg's music that would reward further investigation.

Examining the String Trio, *A Survivor from Warsaw* and the *Phantasy*, pieces that came after the three or four late tonal works, it seems as though they could almost be a reaction to them. In fact these are some of the most radical-sounding of all Schoenberg's pieces, but radical in a different way, because, as Knussen thought, the sound comes from the language "breaking up." The composition method of the violin *Phantasy*, where Schoenberg first wrote the piece for solo violin then added the piano part, is also a symptom of this breaking up of the language.

In contrasting these late works with an earlier masterpiece, *Erwartung* for instance, some of its greatness comes from the fact that it cannot be analyzed or explained in any traditional sense. It seems purely an exercise in stream of consciousness, which is pretty much all you can say about it. The mystery of it is the question of what is so alluring about it. It seems to me to be a piece of the very highest conceivable technical level where all the normal hallmarks of how a thing is done have more or less disappeared. It's impossible to compose music like *Erwartung*. If it was possible, many others would have done it and nobody has. It is important to note that he wrote *Erwartung* very quickly, remarkably in less than a week, and it follows that one of his most complex pieces where you can *see* the technique, the double canon movement in *Pierrot Lunaire*, which really whizzes along, was written in a day and would have required intense focus.

Babbitt and then Alan Forte used this atonal-period method to develop a theoretical system and tried to apply it retrospectively to the music of the past. It was an attempt at finding out how the compositional mind works. It was not an attempt that I can wholeheartedly sympathize with, but the intention was surely to see if the way composers worked was the same regardless of what century they lived in.

One of the seminal Schoenberg events for me as a composer, apart from pushing dots around, was the publication of Schoenberg's *Style and Idea*, which changed the way I thought about the music of the past and the present. I am talking here of the original smaller edition of the book, not the big edition now available. It had an enormous effect on me.

After that was the *Harmonielehre*. Nobody I know has ever used it for teaching harmony, though Schoenberg himself might have done. The central idea of the harmony book, which was written at the very time that tonal practice broke down, is based on the notion of permutability, which has absolutely nothing to do with tonal music. It's a systematic book and I certainly learned from it myself, but I have never taught anyone from it, nor do I think you could teach anyone from it. The best aspect of it is not the harmony, but the asides. I have used parts of the *Structural Functions of Harmony* as a teacher. However, I have never believed that you could teach from Schoenberg's textbooks, and certainly not from the counterpoint book, which I don't like, as I don't think it leads to good counterpoint. What are these books telling us about Schoenberg? Despite the fact that they mostly weren't written as books but edited from lecture notes, I think you can learn much about him as a composer, teacher, and thinker from them.

## 9. ULRICH SIEGELE

It was surely an act of faith—if not of folly—for me to choose Rinuccini's old *Arianna* libretto, when I could barely make out the meaning of the words. Yet I knew it was right for me, just as I would have known that *Orfeo* or *Poppea* or, for that matter, *La Traviata* or *Lohengrin* (had they been so unfortunate as to lose their music) would not be right. I also knew, and this may seem almost perverse, that it was to be *Arianna* and not *Ariadne*—that is, Italian and not English. Common sense led me to experiment with the possibility of an English version, for it would certainly have made things a lot easier; but in this case I knew that my attraction had as much to do with the sound as the meaning of the antique Italian... My final score is deliberately patchy: some parts are highly worked, polyphonically and instrumentally; elsewhere the bare bones of the original are left to stand. The impression I aim to create is one of transparency: the listener should perceive, both in the successive and simultaneous dimensions of the score, the old beneath the new and the new arising from the old. We are to see a mythological and ancient action, interpreted by a seventeenth-century poet in a modern theatre. My hope, as expressed by Rinuccini's Apollo in the (unset) prologue of *Arianna*, is that "it will come to pass that in these new songs you will admire the ancient glory of the Grecian stage."

*(Alexander Goehr, Royal Opera House programme, 1995, for the premiere performances of Arianna)*

*JVZ: One very important aspect of being a composer that Goehr and I both ascribe to is that you never stop learning throughout your lifetime, even long after you have completed any formal educational process or degree work. It is quite common that an experienced professional composer might be influenced by the ideas of a peer, and Goehr's friendship with the German musicologist and Bach scholar Ulrich Siegele, that began in 1974, is surely one of those cases. In fact, the influence of Siegele's work on Goehr's music from that year is still very much evident right up to the present, such is its depth of interest for him.*

*Goehr considers Siegele to be a crucial mentor in his life from the point of view that, at a time when he was looking to go in a different direction, Siegele came along at the right moment and opened his eyes to a whole new way of thinking which was rooted in the unique analysis of Bach's music that has been Siegele's life work. This relationship also stimulated thought and exploration in Goehr's music where seeds were already present, such as his deep love and appreciation of the work of Monteverdi (something else Goehr passed on to me) that was furthered through his discussions with Siegele on the early Baroque master.*

*Many of the ideas and processes that Goehr derived from Siegele's deep dive into the work of Bach and that he describes in this chapter were already present in Goehr's music in some form. The different path, however, that Goehr takes with those areas of interest that are characteristic of his own mechanics as a composer was very much influenced by Siegele's discoveries. Some of these important characteristics we explore in the second part of this book.*

*There is quite a change in Goehr's music in a very short period of time in the mid-1970s that coincided with my arrival as his student and assistant. The change from the serial works of the 1960s and 70s to works based on a more traditional use of musical material created a distinct boundary between two types of music that seemed mind-bogglingly different to me at the time. I couldn't then see the relationship between the earlier works and what was new as a natural evolutionary process. The differences in sound and approach between those last serial works such as* Metamorphosis/Dance, op. 36, Chaconne for Wind Instruments, op. 34, *and* the *Third String Quartet, op. 37, on the one hand, and the* Psalm 4, op. 38 *series as well as the operas* Behold the Sun *and* Arianna *on the other hand, seemed a universe apart to me then—not that I didn't love and appreciate all of those works on some level.*

*Now, of course, I see it all differently and much more clearly, having developed an intimate relationship with almost all of Goehr's works over the years. My way of thinking was that the earlier works which I was so familiar with when I became his student represented a radical, modernist, revolutionary approach, while the works from the* Psalm 4 *series and afterwards were more traditional and somewhat reactionary. I had it exactly backwards though. The works since* Psalm 4, *all of which have in some way been inspired by Goehr's interest in Siegele's Bach investigations, have been products of a much more revolutionary approach, and one that I now can see was ahead of its time. It took great courage for an established composer in his forties to make such a radical change in his music in the mid-1970s. I believe that it was an anxious though conscious choice to pursue the new direction in spite of the misunderstanding it might cause for critics, theorists, and audiences (as well as young student composers). And this, for me, has been an especially important lesson later in my professional life. It proved that we composers never stop learning and can always seek new avenues of exploration without regard to fashion or sometimes harsh criticism from those who have little or no understanding of what it is we do.*

*I believe that the reader will find this chapter of critical importance in understanding Goehr's music and teachings today. It will also shed much light on the subjects we discuss in the next part of this book.*

AG: Around 1973–74, I was much in demand and getting a lot of commissions for substantial pieces, and I wrote several works—*Lyric Pieces, op. 35;* Piano Concerto, *op. 33; Metamorphosis/Dance, op. 36* and the Third String Quartet, op. 37—that were all based on classical models from Mozart, Beethoven, Schumann. The reason for that was that I was very preoccupied with the concept of the duration of pieces. Before that, my post-Webern pieces were rather short, and now that longer "full length" pieces were required of me, I used classical models of proportions and durations in order to discipline myself to write longer lengths.

That technique certainly worked for me in the last of my dodecaphonic pieces where I used twelve-tone rows in my particular adaptations, which was how I had composed for some years. However, I became unhappy with two aspects of the way I was doing things. First, I was depending too much on these classical models; and second, as with writing fugues, when I composed with a twelve-tone row, I knew in advance what it was going to give me, and I had become too familiar with that way of composing.

So this was the state of affairs in the summer of 1974, when I was visited at University of Leeds by Ulrich Siegele, a Bach scholar and professor of musicology from Tübingen University in Germany. His wife, Leonore, a radical theologian who had written a book about the evangelical Protestant church in the time of the Nazis which had been very controversial in Tübingen, had been invited to lecture in England at Leeds and Durham universities on her subject for a term, and he came with her. I asked Ulrich to give lectures to my students at Leeds and we became good friends.

What interested me about his work was his investigation into the durational aspects of Bach's music, such as the use of golden section and other forms of arithmetical applications. He had done a very detailed analysis of the six-part fugal *ricercar* from *The Musical Offering*, which he showed to me. I wondered if these techniques could exist with any form of harmony, i.e., were they part of an abstract system of proportion. He was demonstrating the relationship between motivic harmonic structure and metric proportion in Bach's works, and this became his life's work, culminating in more recent times in his series of four books called *Bach Composes Time*. (Most of Siegele's works are only available in German, and very few of his articles have been translated into English, which is a pity.)

Siegele is a very scholarly man who never generalizes and only talks about what he can demonstrate. His system became very elaborate when he combined the motivic/harmonic factors with metric proportion in his analyses, because sometimes it didn't fit. So he used the terminology which comes from German musicologist Hugo Riemann, which analyzes, for instance, metric proportion in four-bar phrases—so when there is a five-bar phrase, you show it as four plus one, and then match the next phrase of three bars as four minus one, meaning that you keep to the overall proportion even though within these structures the details vary, which he was able to show.

I got very absorbed in his system, and we talked a great deal about it. He introduced me to a book that I owned but had never read, Carl Philipp Emanuel Bach's book about keyboard technique, *Essay on the True Art of Playing Keyboard Instruments*. I wasn't particularly interested in the part of the book about performing, as I am not a performer, but the part about harmonic structure was something else.

When Siegele left Leeds to return to Germany after many discussions of considerable detail, I spent a summer doing the exercises from the C.P.E. Bach book, and inventing my own exercises based on the book, which had very much to do with techniques of reharmonization. For instance, in playing the keyboard in a work, if you have a bass line and a vocal line, you can reharmonize these in very different ways. The simplest example would be the Bach chorales.

I got very involved in this over the summer of 1975, and composed an occasional piece for the funeral service of a friend, a setting of Psalm 4 for solo soprano and alto, women's chorus, viola solo, and organ, my Op. 38a. The piece turned out to be fifteen minutes long as opposed to the required three, so it didn't get performed at the ceremony. It combined for the first time the ideas that I had learned from C.P.E. Bach as well as some I had gleaned from Monteverdi. It led to two further associated pieces, the *Fugue on the notes of Psalm 4, op. 38b,* for string orchestra, and the *Romanza on the notes of Psalm 4, op. 38c,* for two violins and two violas concertante and strings, which is one of my favorites of my pieces.

This was a big change in the way I composed, namely in that it combined much more formal metric ideas derived from Siegele's influence, and this led to a whole new development. During that summer of C.P.E. Bach, I went to the Edinburgh Festival and heard Carlo Maria Guilini do a performance of Beethoven's *Missa Solemnis*, and it caused me to remember that my great friend the choral director John Alldis had said to me that a choral work didn't need to have a great poem, but a great subject.

After the Beethoven performance, I tried and failed to make a text out of Shelley's *Prometheus*, which is on the subject of revolution, but this led to my set of four pieces for mixed choir and orchestra, *Babylon the Great Is Fallen*, and ultimately to my opera *Behold the Sun* (which the choral pieces formed a part of). This was an attempt to deal with a big subject, the biggest I ever dealt with: the Anabaptist uprising in Münster in 1534–5. That focus on the big subject combined with Siegele's work on J. S. Bach and C. P. E. Bach's book were the main influences on me at that time, and they resulted in my new approach and works.

Also at that time, we talked a lot about Monteverdi and how Siegele believed that the *Seconda Prattica*, i.e., the technique of Monteverdi, is based on the *Prima Prattica*, i.e., the style of strict counterpoint of Palestrina, elaborated and ornamented. I said to Siegele, if that's the case, what's to stop me from writing in strict counterpoint like the *Prima Prattica*, and elaborating on it in my own style, as Monterverdi did in his work as per the *Seconda Prattica*? And many years later, my adaptation of this idea became my opera *Arianna* and another of my works, *The Death of Moses, op. 53*. In *Arianna* it was through setting the original Italian text for the lost Monteverdi opera by Ottavio Rinuccini in the version that my Cambridge colleague and friend, professor of Italian Patrick Boyde, read and explained to me. It was his reading of it that I set, and I did exactly as I proposed: I wrote in the strict counterpoint of the *Prima Prattica*, and then elaborated on it in a variety of different ways.

I also wrote a piece in 1985 called … *a musical offering (J.S.B. 1985)*, in which I also composed a six-part *ricercar* (fugue), not based on Frederick the Great's name as Bach's work was, but based on Bach's name. This piece very much used those techniques that I have described.

Siegele's influence on me lasted a very long time. In those few months that he was in Leeds and we frequently met, he actually altered my whole direction as a composer. We are still friends, and we have visited each other regularly over the years and have gone on discussing these subjects. His life's work is now very considerable.

Like I said, Siegele is not one to generalize. If he talks about the *Goldberg Variations*, the *48 Preludes and Fugues*, or *The Art of the Fugue*, etc., he does so by analyzing each particular one methodically and systematically. It's not everybody's taste—it's hard going at times—but one interesting aspect of it is that he says he writes primarily for composers, not musical historians. In that sense, he is one of my mentors and he has had a profound influence on me of a very considerable kind that has lasted right up to the present. It's the way I work now—for better or worse.

Siegele presents his analyses in tabular form. He deals with the motivic and harmonic aspects of the pieces—in fugues, variations, etc., and genres and types—but because this is presented very systematically, it is very hard to read. He is very precise with the numbers of measures, the textures, etc. For instance, in the *48 Preludes and Fugues* and the *ricercar* from *The Musical Offering*, he presents and discusses the proportional relationship between sections where the fugue subject is present, and where it is not. He discovered that there is an important proportional relationship between those two types of episodes, and these involve harmonic as well as metric proportion. It's mostly metric, but there are places where Bach will be making continual variations on one harmonic sequence that doesn't end in the right place, and he'll go on for two more measures, say, but he will make up for it by shortening another variation so that the overall proportions remain the same.

In order to do this kind of analysis, Siegele must work out the tempi of Bach's pieces, which is difficult as there are no metronome indications or specific tempo marks in Bach's scores. However, Bach had sixty-minute hourglass sand clocks on his organ, and because he was writing music to fit Lutheran services, he had to work much as a film composer does today. Lutheran services were measured exactly in hours and minutes. In order for a work—a cantata for instance—composed for a service to finish at the right time, a certain number of pieces had to be in a fixed tempo to give him a known duration. Siegele found out that the tempi were related to the types of movements—*alla breve*, slow, dance, etc.—and he worked out by very complex mathematics what the tempi had to be in each of them, because without knowing the tempi, the time proportions and relationships wouldn't mean anything. In his analysis system, where there are chorales, he considers them presented in whole notes, recitatives twice as fast, and various types of choruses and arias in different tempi according to genre. As you can imagine, this yields a very complex structure. You would never hear it performed this way because nobody knows it, and if any of Bach's pieces *were* preformed like that, the audience would reject this, because it's not the way the performance tradition of his music since Mendelssohn has worked. So it remains a historical theoretical concept.

One of the things that impressed me most in what Siegele told me was the Aristotelian conception of the "whole" which he believed applied to Bach's method of composition, where you think of the total duration of a piece first, and then you divide that whole. This is the only way to obtain fixed durations. You couldn't do it additively.

Since Siegele has shown that Bach worked this way in the *Goldberg Variations*, the cantatas, and the B Minor Mass, it seems likely that he always composed that way, and that these numerical relationships in musical works had to be part of the compositional technique of that time. It is known that Bach (as well as Handel) was a member of polymath Lorenz Mizler's Corresponding Society of the Musical Sciences, which explored the intersections of mathematics and music. It appears that this technique was a great secret that Bach, Handel, and other composers knew, but never told anyone about!

Thinking that this is perhaps related to the mysterious techniques of creating sequences of stained glass, Siegele spent some time pacing around gothic cathedrals and Palladian houses in Italy to try and discover their proportional structures. Certainly if you measure cathedrals you find that their structures follow certain proportional systems. They would have to, otherwise they wouldn't stand up! The comparison between mathematical proportions like those in cathedrals and musical structure excited me very much and made me want to compose.

Many composers would have probably just shrugged their shoulders and said, "Big deal. So that's just the way Bach did it." (However, Max Davies was very enthusiastic when I told him about it, as was Elliott Carter.) Siegele didn't know that many composers and I introduced him to a few later on the few occasions he came to Cambridge, but he didn't have the profound effect on them that he had on me. I am sure that one of the reasons I took to this method was that I was ready for something like this to come along in my life; I was fertile ground, so to speak. It is true that this way of thinking had similarities to the way I worked already, and probably made me a perfect fit for Siegele's ideas.

You do find many of these techniques in medieval and Renaissance music, where there was a combining of theology with musical practice. However, Siegele would not have been interested in the idea that this method in Bach was an abstraction. He would see it as part of Bach's belief system, and Bach, especially in his organ works, deliberately took elements out of the scriptures, and used those images as structural devices. Siegele was more in sympathy with the much despised approach of Albert Schweitzer, which was based on the relationship between theology and proportion to some extent, but in a much less precise way.

One aspect of this subject that is of great interest to me is the relationship between that sort of planning, which is implied in the Aristotelian proportional concept, and improvisation. You can't visualize a composition without some arbitrary improvisational invented element. And that, by its very nature, doesn't necessarily fit into a fixed duration, and the relationship between an improvised fragment and a proportional system is what inspired me and kept me going over the years. However, now that I have gotten older, I don't have the energy to devise the proportional systems anymore and just do the improvisation part! But this did not happen to Bach. There is no evidence that he ever stopped composing in this way.

One of the things that Siegele told me that I find interesting is that at the time when Bach was a schoolboy, they were still using old-fashioned Catholic schoolbooks because the Lutherans didn't yet have any of their own. One important aspects of this would have been Bach's study of rhetoric. A basic principle of rhetoric is the relationship between the greater part and the lesser part. The Bach works that Siegele has analyzed always follow that tradition of the rhetoric. The basic concept of this is that you present your ideas in a smaller part and develop them in a greater part. Of course that happens in all music, and it's the kind of simplification and generalization of the kind that Siegele wouldn't approve of—to describe what, in fact, is a very elaborate and precise manner of operating which is different in all sorts of works. It must also be remembered that in Bach's time, all music, even improvised music, operated within a convention much more narrowly defined than anything we would understand. It was very much like table manners: you put your fork on the left and your knife on the right!

*Ulrich Siegele, 2022. Photo by Linda Koldau*

# INTERLUDE
# THE AMERICAN EXPERIENCE

## 10. WOLPE, COPLAND, CARTER, SESSIONS, SCHULLER AND BABBITT

*JVZ: Over the years, Goehr has had close relationships with many American composers. He has a great appreciation of American culture, which began with his first trip to the U.S. as a young composer. Since then, he has traveled widely around the country and has had commissions and performances from coast to coast. He taught at the New England Conservatory of Music in Boston, and at Yale University, where he was offered a permanent appointment, as well as Tanglewood, Aspen, and Marlboro. Many American composers have studied with him, either in these institutions, or having traveled to study with him at Cambridge in the decades that he was Professor of Music there. Some of them were my colleagues Joan Huang, Daria Semegen, David Froom, Harold Meltzer, David Babcock, and Joseph Landers. American music has made its mark on him as he has made his mark on American music, a very fair trade.*

JVZ: *You went to America for the first time in the early 1960s, is that right?*

AG: Yes. On my first visit in 1962, it was arranged that I be taken to lunch by Aaron Copland. At that time, I was no great admirer of his music (though I am now) and I knew he had served on a committee that had not given a grant to Schoenberg to complete *Moses and Aron*. The meeting was not a great success. But as we were parting on a pavement near the Lincoln Center, he said to me, "You know, it's not easy to grow old as a composer. If you start imitating newer fashions you make a fool of yourself. If you stick to what you can do, you become passé and out of date." I was moved by this, coming from one of the most successful composers in the world, and felt very small.

*Alexander Goehr 1960s. Photo by Laelia Goehr*

On that first trip, I spent some time at Princeton. I had previously met Edward T. Cone, whom I stayed with and whose writings I very much admired, and I went to a few classes given by Roger Sessions and Milton Babbitt, both of whose music I very much liked. Possibly, in this context, I could say that Babbitt was a kind of mentor. Of this more later. Sessions is neglected nowadays, but I enjoyed his work.

JVZ: *I agree. When I was a young student in the early 1970s, Sessions's music was everywhere. Alas, he seems to have almost completely disappeared off the radar. This has happened to some other very good American composers, George Crumb for instance, who after a period of great success disappeared from the national scene for more than twenty years. Now his pieces are being enthusiastically performed again everywhere by a new generation. So perhaps Sessions will have a comeback some day.*

AG: Well, I hope so. He wrote a very good Violin Concerto, and the *Idyll of Theocritus* for soprano and orchestra (I seem to recall that it owed something to *Erwartung*), as well as some striking operas: *Montezuma* and an un-Brechtian *Trial of Lucullus*. I remained in touch with Sessions over the years, both in the U.S. and England.

In New York, I also found Stefan Wolpe, to whom I had been very attracted in Darmstadt, and I saw a great deal of him, right up till his death in 1972. By contrast to anyone else (with the exception of his pupil Ralph Shapey), he was the original rebel.

JVZ: *I also admire his music, but I don't think anyone in my generation and after knows anything about him. What was he like as a person?*

AG: His rebelliousness was infectious. He was unlike many artists, not at all withdrawn, and he was very physical as, indeed, is his music. When he showed you a score of his own, he would put it in front of you and then proceed to perform it from beginning to end with rough imitations of phrases, onomatopoeic noises, grunts, and yells, etc. In Paris he had suggested I copy his big symphony (I earned a living as a copyist for some years), but I soon gave it back to him, because the notation was pretty crazy: compound measures of differing units (7/16+1/4+2/8) but with each instrument acting independently of the measure. When later I heard Frederik Prausnitz performing it with the BBC Orchestra, I could make little of it, though I've heard a recording since

**151**

which is very striking. What I do realize is that Wolpe is a kind of "speaking composer." Like the man himself, his music is very immediate and physical in effect, and is a kind of extended monody. This probably explains his success as a teacher of jazz musicians (among others) and his influence on Cage. Once, sitting in a café in Finchley Road, London, looking at an ashtray full of butts, he said, "Look at this—just like new music: all different and all the same!"

JVZ: *Wolpe is another composer whose chamber music you used to hear quite often, but don't any longer. I have never seen an orchestral piece by him programmed that I can remember.*

AG: He wrote mostly chamber ensemble pieces and only the one symphony. There's an excellent recording of his piece for piano and ensemble with Peter Serkin, conducted by Oliver Knussen. But generally, in his lifetime, his performances were not good.

JVZ: *Did that have something to do with his notation, do you think?*

AG: Possibly the notation, but he also had bad luck.

JVZ: *One of your best American composer friends was Gunther Schuller. What kind of relationship did you have with him?*

AG: He was my closest American friend. I met him originally at Darmstadt, where we both had a piece performed. His was a very good piece called *Dramatic Overture*. It was booed, not because anyone particularly disliked it, but because the orchestra had refused to play Stravinsky's *Ebony Concerto*, on the grounds that it was jazz and they weren't able to play it, which is probably true. The Stravinsky was taken off the program, and as a result, the audience booed the end of the concert, and unfortunately the last piece was Schuller's. He came up to me afterwards when he heard me speaking English with Harry Birtwistle, to ask us why they booed it. I explained to him what it was about and that it had nothing to do with his piece. And from that time on, which goes back to the 1950s, we were good friends. He stayed with us in London, and when I went to America the first time I stayed with him and his dear wife, Margie. He was a wonderful musician and I learned a great deal from him. I liked his early pieces very much, and because he was a great horn player, he wrote extraordinarily interesting music for brass. His famous Brass Symphony is really remarkable for the textures and sounds he invented. And his *Five Pieces for Horns* is wonderful too.

Gunther was extremely generous in word and deed. He was eager to hear and perform music of all kinds, and his tastes were broad: jazz, Delius, Babbitt, and the whole range of classical and romantic repertoire. As first horn of the Metropolitan Opera Orchestra, he knew his operas. He was extremely fluent as a composer. He would sit at his kitchen table, jazz on the radio, turning out orchestral commissions as others make pancakes.

At first, very enthusiastic about the Schoenberg School, he considered that it was his function as a composer to make new techniques available and comprehensible to the general run of players, and he did this very successfully. He was extremely versatile: he worked as a writer, teacher, organizer, conductor, and jazz musician, as well as producing compositions one after the other.

There is a potential hazard in excessive fluency, with Milhaud and Villa-Lobos being prime examples. It often affects performers. Gunther's ideas were striking, but once realized, he (like others) became a prisoner of process. He adopted methods of construction derived from Schoenberg as seen through the eyes of Babbitt. There, he used the combinatorial principle developed by Babbitt, but turned it from a self-sufficient mode of thought, positivist in limitation, to a tool or process of generating material and joining it with, or using it in, connection with a broader musical activity. As an illustration of this, it is interesting to compare any of Gunther's "Third Stream" jazz-classical synthesis pieces with Babbitt's austere *All Set* for jazz musicians.

JVZ: All Set is *one of Babbitt's very best pieces in my opinion, and it anticipated the advanced jazz of the 1960s. Many people don't realize that he was a jazz fan and was even known to play jazz piano gigs on occasion.*

AG: He also knew and tried his hand at the American musicals of Broadway, though not, it seems, with great success. When he illustrated a point in class at the piano, he would include "popular" harmony in his example. As for his own compositions, they repay careful study. Unlike Boulez and the Darmstadt composers, he saw in the method of twelve notes a limited but endlessly adaptable way of combining pitch levels, durational values, and dynamics which is, in aspiration, a language (as is claimed for Webern). Probably Babbit's best work involved electronic composition undertaken at the Columbia-Princeton studio, where he was able to fully realize his detailed compositions. Apart from occasional good performances—such as the Cleveland Orchestra's performance of *Relata II*, conducted by Gunther Schuller, and Levine and the Boston Symphony Orchestra's performance of *Concerti*—they were often an approximation. Oliver Knussen would not perform his work, because he considered it unrealizable.

However, Babbitt had a fine ear. I remember him, despairing at a rehearsal of *Relata II* with the Scottish National Orchestra. No doubt it was such an approximation that he considered it hopeless. He wouldn't even suggest corrections. Yet on repeated listening, something came across, at least in part. Babbitt would have regarded whatever his audience got from it as trivial. If listeners couldn't perceive the intended notes, durations, instrumental dynamics, there was nothing else.

JVZ: *Well, of course another thing about Babbitt, like Sessions, is that he taught for so long at Princeton that the United States is full of his pupils. His influence really does live on, even though his music isn't played that much anymore.*

AG: Well, that seems to be the fate of yesterday's music. It has to be replaced by today's. I certainly don't share what appears to me to be Babbitt's limited view of what music is. However, I would acknowledge a line of thinking—Schoenberg, Krenek, late Stravinsky, and Babbitt—which has inspired the way I developed my own practice, at least up to a certain point.

JVZ: *Let's turn to Elliott Carter. I know you were good friends and over the years, you've made some interesting comments about his music to me. I just wonder, in considering his legacy now, what you think about him.*

AG: I don't know what his legacy will be, but I hope he won't suffer the same neglect as have the others I've mentioned here. Some of his pieces will surely be of interest in the future. As seems to be my own taste, I particularly admire pieces which represent a move from past to future, leaving traces of both in some kind of a synthesis: Stravinsky's *Agon* and *Canticum Sacrum*, Beethoven all the time (!), Schoenberg's *Jakobsleiter*, and Bartók's Third String Quartet. I particularly admire Carter's First String Quartet displaying a kind of Beethovenian moral purpose, the Double Concerto for Harpsichord and Piano, and the Variations for Orchestra, and later the Concerto for Orchestra. And then there is the influence of Charles Ives. Gunther Schuller had done a remarkable version of Ives's Fourth Symphony, and I became fascinated and moved by his music and ideas.

JVZ: *It was a huge thing for American music when Ives was rediscovered. I think Elliott Carter, who knew Ives for many years, had something to do with his rebirth, if I remember correctly.*

AG: Well yes and no. Carter, I noticed, was quite dismissive of "Mr. Ives," as he called him, whom he had known and who had encouraged him as a young man. "All derived from Debussy's *Fetes*," he said rather disparagingly. But I find traces of Ives' influence, particularly in the Second String Quartet and the Duo for Violin and Piano. In his systematic fastidious way, like Boulez, he probably rejected Ives's harmony as a bit hit-or-miss. Many composers are negative about their influences, and I don't think they are always subconscious influences. I remember a story about what Britten would do when he was having a hard time composing. He disliked Brahms so much that if he played some of his music, it made him angry enough that he then started composing himself!

I also think Carter must have been influenced by the theoretical books of Joseph Schillinger (*Schillinger Method of Musical Composition* and *The Mathematical Basis of the Arts*). Many of Carter's notions about rhythmic construction (metric modulation) and orchestration seem to have some relationship to Schillinger's ideas. But Carter denied this when I asked him about it. I wonder whether his friend Conlon Nancarrow wasn't also influenced by Schillinger?

JVZ: *Did you ever find something in the Schillinger that helped you in any way, or gave you any new ideas?*

AG: Not directly. Richard Hall in Manchester was very interested in Schillinger and I read his books at that time. I was amused when I saw the film *The Glenn Miller Story*: Glenn Miller comes out of the stage door and says to his wife, "Have you met Dr. Schillinger?" That is almost as good as Wagner beginning *Tristan* at the top of a large sheet of music paper in the piccolo part! But seriously, Schillinger's most distinguished pupil was Gershwin, whose notebooks analyzing Stravinsky, Schoenberg, and others according to the Schillinger method are in the Library of Congress. As far as I know, nobody has studied them. His many pupils were often eminent jazz musicians and arrangers of big band music. The only direct pupil of his I knew was Earle Brown.

JVZ: *I'd like to talk to you a little bit about when you came to the U.S. again in the late 1960s and you spent a year teaching at the New England Conservatory, after which you had an associate professorship at Yale. You've also done Tanglewood three times, as well as Aspen, and Marlboro.*

AG: Well, it was the first time I had taught in educational institutions and was called professor, which I found embarrassing. The New England Conservatory and Boston–Cambridge was fascinating, and apart from being with Schuller a great deal, there was the conductor Fred Prausnitz, the violinist Joe Silverstein, the composer Leon Kirschner (at Harvard), and many others. Yale was less interesting (except that it was nearer to New York), and then it was closed down early in 1968 by student unrest, making it too short a time for me to really do the job. Teaching composition is a chancy business at the best of times, like throwing a ball in the air and hoping someone catches it!

JVZ: *And did being in America have any influence on your own pieces?*

AG: Yes, but who knows what it was exactly. My principal work in those years was my *Symphony in One Movement*, and it seems to me that its density of texture probably reflects the atmosphere of America. I was certainly more attuned to America than to Darmstadt. Darmstadt was like a political party: you almost had to wear a badge to belong. In America, or at least in the circle I knew, there was a broader culture. The performing outlets were possibly more conventional than in Germany at that time, but standards were spectacular. It was a different cultural climate, and it was more attuned to syntheses rather than the iconoclasm of Darmstadt.

*JVZ: You haven't mentioned Varèse. We are both great admirers of his music. You once told me you visited him in New York. What was that like?*

AG: Yes, I went with Luigi Nono to Varèse's beautiful house. He was a great man and, as you say, I admired his music (in fact my father had recorded *Integrales* in the 1930s). It was like visiting an old monument. He was a bit drunk and confused me with my Uncle Rudy, whom he also knew. The house was full of exotic musical instruments. The famous Mrs. Varèse was also there.

You never visit a composer's house without learning something about them you didn't know: Puccini's in Torre del Lago, Janáček's in Brno, Schoenberg's in Los Angeles. It was this way with Varèse too. I asked him what he was composing.

He answered, "A text by Anaïs Nin."
"What's it about?" I asked.
"Cunts," he answered.

*JVZ: Can you tell me about the first performance of* Colossos or Panic, op. 55, *in 1993 by the Boston Symphony Orchestra conducted by Seiji Ozawa?*

AG: I loved having my music played in that hall which has an acoustic—like at Dresden or the Moscow Conservatoire—that gives music a particular quality. My piece *Colossos or Panic*, after a painting by Goya, sounded almost like Ravel there. It surprised me because it was not how I had imagined it would sound.

*JVZ: Do you remember what the reaction was to the piece in Boston?*

AG: Not really. Polite, I suppose. I do remember being interviewed by the critic of the *Boston Globe* and at the end he said, "When I hear your music, I wonder why it's not performed more. When I hear what you say about music, I wonder that it's performed at all!"

# PART II
## MODELS AND EXPLORATIONS

## 11. MODELING

JVZ: *You have told me that a number of your works were modeled on pieces from the past that inspired you, such as the Finale of Mozart's* Jupiter Symphony. *The most obvious example to the average listener might be your opera* Arianna, *where you composed your own re-creation of the lost Monteverdi opera from the surviving libretto. But in other works,* Metamorphosis/Dance, *for instance, the effects of modeling are not readily detectable without a detailed analysis. Can you explain how this concept works in your compositional process?*

AG: You can divide the subject of modeling into two areas. One is when you recreate in some way something that already exists, and the other is what I call the "antiquarian" aspect. For instance, one may be inspired by Bach fugues, the finale of the *Jupiter* Symphony, or Schumann and Monteverdi, like I have, and then create a relationship with the past through imitating these models in some way. The antiquarian side of it would probably be looked at with some suspicion by a lot of people who would regard this as an unnecessary homage to tradition. For me the only justification for the use of models is when they allow me to do something new that I hadn't been able to do before.

The way that a model works is widely varied. It can be a general inspiration, i.e., nothing specific, or it can be a system of echoing the exact proportions of a model piece. Around the time of the composition of my Piano Concerto and Third String Quartet, I was concerned to get the durations right for the material, so I modeled my pieces on quite specific movements from late Beethoven piano sonatas, Mozart piano concertos, etc.

At a certain point I felt that my attitude towards the subject of models was too mechanical, and that I was more concerned with the physical detail of a model while I ignored the musical content. Obviously, if you want to imitate the musical content or the nature of the contrasts of tempi, harmony, etc., in a model, that's a somewhat vaguer procedure. You can count the number of bars in a movement and divide it up as I would do, being very much under the influence of Ulrich Siegele's work on Bach that we have discussed. I did that and used proportions rather like what painters do. They sit in front of a painting at the Louvre or National Gallery, they divide their canvas into squares, then they fill in the squares according to the painting they are using as a model, holding their pencil forward in perspective in order to get the proportions right. They calculate the size of the figures then realize them on their own terms.

That is classical educational modeling for painters, as you can read about in Richard Wollheim's great book, *Painting as an Art*, which provided the basis for what I have written on the subject. The young Manet and Cézanne were well known to be frequent visitors to the Louvre to do that sort of copying. Gradually that practice turned into something original. For instance, Cézanne's painting *The Bathers*, which was made in this way (and has several developing versions), is an imitation of a Renaissance painting.

One of the issues of modeling that Wollheim is very keen on, is whether you are meant to see (or hear in music) the model through the result of the new painting. That issue of "transparency" also concerns me, because sometimes I wanted it to appear in my piece. For instance in my opera *Arianna*, I wanted Monteverdi to be a "presence," even though I was trying to write original music.

JVZ: *When did you discover that you could do this?*

AG: In a sense it was always there. I had looked closely at my father's copy of Brahms's *Handel Variations* which he annotated in Schoenberg's class with his teacher's analytical remarks, and this may have given me some idea of it. In a way I was always trying to use models in my pieces, although not very systematically, and not very sensibly early on. When I was at the Conservatoire with Messiaen, and I wrote my analysis of the Finale of Mozart's *Jupiter* Symphony, detailing its combination of homophonic and fugal techniques, it was largely influenced by an analysis of the same movement by the Austrian music theorist Simon Sechter, who taught Anton Bruckner. My analysis, which won the *deuxième prix*, the foreigner's top prize at the Conservatoire, was described by Messiaen as being "very personal." I found his view strange because it seemed to me that it was anything but that, but it was personal to him, probably because it was not the sort of thing that anyone did at the Conservatoire!

After that I began what became my First String Quartet, and I modeled it on the *Jupiter* finale in its combinatorial counterpoint. It bears no aural relationship to the Mozart, and if I didn't say it, no one would notice it by hearing or even by analysis. It wouldn't cross anyone's mind because it was a general idea rather than a specific one. I then took models as a general idea for some time, on and off whenever I wanted to. It was only much later, really at the end of my twelve-tone period, that I actually started consciously using models. Not the *Little Symphony* or *Symphony in One Movement*, nor the *Romanza for Cello and Orchestra*, but the quasi-serial pieces I wrote immediately before *Psalm 4*: the Piano Concerto, *Metamorphosis/Dance*, and the Third String Quartet. I was consciously taking particular movements and imitating them while trying to make something new out of them. I did feel quite guilty about it and sometimes thought I was overdoing it. When I composed *Psalm 4* without a model, I was relieved that I wasn't doing it anymore. I did do it sometimes later on, but never as consciously or specifically as at that time in

165

those pieces from the early 1970s when I was professor at the University of Leeds.

The first thing that I took from the existing pieces was the proportions between sections of the particular movement I was working from. At that time I had the opportunity to prepare and conduct quite a number of Webern's songs with instruments and small ensembles. I noticed that when we rehearsed them, if we were spending a couple of hours on a set of songs trying to get it right, that as we proceeded, the notes became as big as footballs. I became intensely aware of the quality of the music. Everything seemed to fit together meaningfully, and yet, when we rehearsed the same piece again the following day, we began from scratch, as if we were back at zero and didn't know what we were doing. And again, the same thing would grow on us over the rehearsal.

From that, I thought, "Poor audience who are going to have to sit through this, they'll have no idea what marvelous pieces these are because they are simply so short. They won't be able to get into them." I had the feeling that there was some disparity between duration and material, and that a composer has to work to get the proper length for the material he uses in order to be perceived; otherwise it simply doesn't work in real time. So I was using models to help me do that. That was my original motivation, and of course, that determined how the musical material and the durations would be in balance with one another, which I did by counting out bars.

JVZ: *What made you pick a particular piece for a model, for example as in* Metamorphosis/Dance?

AG: *Metamorphosis/Dance* is based on the second movement of Beethoven's Piano Sonata no. 32, op. 111, a variation movement where each successive variation gets proportionally faster than the one before. However, I reversed the procedure in my piece, and each successive variation slows down from the fastest point and goes back to the original tempo. I counted the bars of each section in the Beethoven, and in my piece I duplicated those same proportions, but I reversed them.

It sometimes has irregularities. Siegele, for instance, when he was talking about proportion in Bach, say in the six-part *ricercar* of the *Musical Offering* (which I also used as a model later on), where there are six-measure phrases, but the melody and harmony didn't fit in a particular phrase and it needed an extra bar in order to adequately finish it, he would call that phrase "six plus one" bars, which would require that there was a "six minus one" section at some other point in the piece to balance things.

JVZ: *What about other elements of a model: texture, orchestration, a general musical idea, etc.? Did these enter into the picture at all?*

AG: They probably did, but I don't know whether you could isolate model from influence in those elements because they are not quantifiable in quite the same way. These are sound qualities. Probably someone with a better ear and knowledge of the repertoire than I have might be able to imitate an actual orchestral sound, but it's not something that I would normally do. The theme of the first movement of my *Little Symphony* had its origin in the "Catacombs" movement of Mussorgsky's *Pictures at an Exhibition*. It was not modeling as such, but an imitation—not exact—of the character of the Mussorgsky movement.

One of the origins of modeling was a visit I made with Max Davies and Harry Birtwistle to an exhibition in the 1950s where we saw the many variations that Picasso made from Velázquez, Goya, and others that were in the show. They had an enormous effect on all three of us, especially Max, who took it up right away as a basis of composition. I came around to it more slowly, and Harry only did it once, in his *The World Is Discovered*, a rather nice piece where he used Heinrich Isaac's *canzonas* as models.

JVZ: *Did your interest in the theoretical writings of Paul Klee have any bearing on your use of models at all?*

AG: No, it's a completely different thing. The one who got interested in Klee and wrote a book about it was Boulez, as it was akin to the idea of abolishing the music of the past and starting again. It was very much a Darmstadt-type idea, and it had an effect on me as well. However, it's the complete opposite of the idea of modeling. I can't see any connection. It's not modeling but cultural influence.

My use of modeling in recent years has been more occasional. In the 1970s, it's what I was doing in every piece. Since then, I sometimes model, like my *... a musical offering (J. S. B. 1985)... op. 46,* for chamber ensemble that uses Bach's six-part *ricercar*, and my *... second musical offering (GFH 2001)..., op. 71,* for orchestra that is a rewriting of a particular piece of Handel's from the Suites.

Another case of modeling more to the point was when I wrote the piece for Peter Serkin, *Marching to Carcassonne, op.74,* which operated on the equation that when anything reappeared, it was half the length it had been before—a sort of *ritornello* idea based on a centipede, or the tale of the tortoise and the hare. Every time the refrain reappears, it's half as long as the last time, until finally it's only one note! It's like Zeno's paradox, I suppose. In order to do that, I felt I had to use something that was recognizable each time it comes up, because there is no point in using such an idea if nobody hears it. So I modeled the refrain piece exactly on a Mozart march from one of the *Notturnos*. I took Mozart's march and I used it precisely, but on my own terms, and I felt that in that way it would be recognized.

My set of piano pieces, *Symmetry Disorders Reach, op. 73*, is another work of this type. This is meant as a didactic work, so I had the pieces that I used as models, by Handel, Schumann, etc., printed at the end of the score, as I felt they ought to be included for educational purposes. In fact, all of my modeled pieces could be seen as didactic. The critic Hans Keller once commented to me that "I very much admire your compositions, but I do get fed up being told how to compose."

JVZ: *Is there a practical argument to be made, saying whatever works in helping you to compose is OK and there is nothing wrong with it?*

AG: Well there is something wrong with it if you don't achieve something new! Of course, I wasn't the first person to do such a thing. Brahms was the first composer to do it where one is consciously aware of it. You might think that the medieval concept of parody is a kind of modeling, but it's a completely different thing and doesn't really apply. You might also think the obvious modern precursor for this kind of composing is Stravinsky. However, I think that Stravinsky modeled less than it would appear.

I discussed this subject with Charles Rosen quite a lot, and he got very interested in it and eventually wrote an article about modeling. He found a short gigue by Mozart that was an exact imitation of one by Bach, and he went on to show how various pieces of Brahms were modeled on Schubert, Beethoven, and, above all, Chopin. Rosen carried this out on his own terms, and being extraordinary and more able than I would be to do this, he located the nature of a model and where it came from. He claimed that the last three piano sonatas by Schubert were based on Beethoven's Op. 31. I didn't see it, but he did, and I believe him.

Now, in my later years, I am employing modeling much less. I am more interested in improvisatory techniques, certainly as far as the material is concerned. My modeling now is not nearly as systematic as it was in earlier years, and I also feel, at this point, that I have written over 100 pieces and that's probably enough! I am probably not going to do it any longer anyway.

JVZ: *I understand why you feel improvisation is a more interesting thing to do. I think you get to the point where if you try and let too much outside stimulus into a piece, that you can get stuck, whereas if you just let it flow naturally, it makes it easier to compose.*

AG: Certainly that's part of it, but there is another reason, I am afraid, and that's that I am no longer physically capable of composing, say a seven or eight minute movement, and sustaining it. I simply do not have the physical energy to do it. Therefore, I mostly write pieces that are two or three minutes long, and I compile lots of short ones into a longer piece. Song cycles are a good bet for me, and I look to *Die Winterreise*, which stands as tall as any symphony, but, of course, it too is composed of many short pieces.

JVZ: *It certainly does take a lot of energy to compose music, and we composers must divert all that we have into doing it when we are working. Of course, I have frequently employed modeling in composing music for TV and film, where it is very common to do so, and have used it in a couple of my concert pieces in the past with interesting results. It can be a very good teaching tool as well. Whenever one of my students is stuck, I often suggest they try a form of modeling, and if they have the ability, they do it and it often works in getting them back to fluency.*

AG: Picasso said that we shouldn't look for things, we should find them. Anyone who goes to the library looking for texts or models is likely to get themselves into trouble! You have to be struck with an idea for it to work. I often dream pieces, and recently I dreamt a piece consisting entirely of adagios, and in the dream, it was by Shostakovich. In fact there is a string quartet by Shostakovich that is all adagios. But then in the dream, I realized it wasn't Shostakovich at all, but Haydn's *Seven Last Words of Our Savior From the Cross*. I woke up about 4 am after this dream, and I got up because I couldn't remember how the Haydn piece worked. So I listened to it from around 4:30 until 5:15 am, had a coffee, and then sat down and started writing a piece that has seven adagios with an allegro at the end, like the Haydn.

Of course, Christ's seven last words wouldn't be appropriate for me, so I replaced them with quotations from Confucius. You have to have something to break it up; otherwise it becomes a continuous piece. So there are spoken parts in between each of the seven adagios. The piece is called *The Master Says, op. 99*, for speaker and chamber orchestra, because each paragraph of *The Analects of Confucius* begins with that phrase. So, that is a different kind of modeling.

I used another type of modeling in my recent piano piece, *Variations in Homage to Haydn, op. 93*, which is based on a set of variations by Haydn that I have always loved, where he juxtaposed sections in major and minor. What's so striking about them is they begin as formal variations in the conventional sense, but then halfway through, they become *sturm und drang* wild improvisations. Then at the end, they return to the more formal, tidy world of the first section. I was excited by the concept, and in my piano piece I imitated the effect and the idea.

## 12. MODALITY

*JVZ: When I first came to you as your student in late 1976, you had just recently written the three* Psalm 4, op. 38 *pieces. Like many others who knew your music at the time, I found this seemingly abrupt change of style in your music to be a mystery; a little bit of a shock really. At the time it didn't make sense to me, but, of course, now it seems completely logical and I have a different view. The reason I bring them up is that these three Opus 38 pieces, to me, were a big turning point in your music and are absolutely central to how you developed afterwards. You have said to me that you don't think of them as being that different from what you were doing before and that it was just a new way of approaching your work. I can see that because in my way of thinking you had always been what I would call a "cantus firmus" composer, and the Op. 38 pieces use the associated* Psalm 4 *modal Gregorian chant in place of the twelve-tone "modes" of your earlier pieces.*

*Where were you in your life as a composer in the mid-1970s, and what was it that inspired you to compose the* Psalm 4 *pieces?*

AG: I was living near Leeds in 1975 in the gatehouse of a stately home in the marvelous countryside, and the wife of the couple who owned it died. The bereaved husband asked could I compose something for his wife's memorial service. The pieces I had recently written at that time, the Third String Quartet, *Metamorphosis/Dance,* and the Piano Concerto, were composed using the dodecaphonic technique that I had been working with for years. From a technical point of view, I felt a little tired of that technique. For instance, if you write fugues, after a certain amount of experience, you can predict what kind of piece it will be from the subject you invent. By analogy, I similarly felt that I could predict what would happen in a piece from the twelve-tone material I invented for it. I was tired of that approach and I felt it was some sort of sign that I should do something new. As I have said before, every once in a while artists must take their clothes off and go naked, and start again, as it were!

That brings me to the composition of the first of the *Psalm 4* pieces for solo soprano and alto, women's chorus, viola solo, and organ. I used the fourth psalm because it is a funeral psalm, and my piece follows a fairly clear-cut pattern that is easily discernible. In the end, the piece wasn't used in the service because what was wanted was a two- or three-minute piece, and what I wrote was a fifteen-minute piece, but it was done shortly afterwards in a concert.

I used the Psalm 4 associated Gregorian chant, which is in the mixolydian mode on G, to make my piece. Now there are two things to consider here. One is that the mode of the chant is "white note," and two, it is common material and I could sing it, which is more than I could do with the twelve-tone rows I invented! I thought that common material is something that I ought to concern myself with as I had not used it in such a direct manner before.

Ex. 3a. Cantus from Psalm 4, op. 38a

The plan of *Psalm 4* is quite simple. It consists of repetitions of the first verse separated by episodes. The verse is repeated eight or ten times, and each time the accompanying line in counterpoint gradually evolves from harmonizing the modal verse in natural "white" notes to chromatic "black" notes (using the analogy of "white" and "black" notes as on the keyboard, but of course my piece has nothing to do with the keyboard). In the middle point, the two-part structure reaches its most contrasted white/black point, and then it gradually reverses itself to the end, where it's back to being all white in both parts.

Ex. 3b. Psalm 4 cantus with "white note" harmony

Ex. 3c. Psalm 4 cantus with "black note" harmony

Each two-part structure is then freely harmonized by me according to no particular principle. (As I have already told you, at that time I was inventing exercises for myself analogous to C.P.E. Bach's harmony exercises in his book *The Art of Keyboard Playing*.) The repeating two-part verse for chorus is followed by four- or five-part variations for the viola and organ which include the two voices from the previous choral section. Then in between those verse repetitions and variations, there are freely composed episodes for the solo soprano and alto. Each time through, I introduced more chromatic notes as I was moving from "white" to "black."

In order to get from one mode that is all white to one that has one chromatic note, on the analogy of episodes in fugues,

I invented freely, and in each subsequent episode I introduced one more chromatic note. So it was a fairly composite structure, and quite a simple one. It ought to be easily audible if you are listening for that. And that is more or less the structure of *Psalm 4, op. 38a.* It was an occasional piece, but when I had finished it, it didn't let me go. So I then wrote a version of it, *Romanza on the Notes of Psalm 4, op. 38c,* for two solo violins, two solo violas and string orchestra, where I took the identical structure of the Psalm, but elaborated on it with decorations of a Baroque kind. Then I took it and wrote *Fugue on the Notes of Psalm 4, op. 38b,* for string orchestra. It sounds like a fugue though it really isn't one, but it is a rearrangement of Op. 38a, and it has a ritornello where the two-part structures of the original are recombined in different ways.

So I made a kind of triptych of the pieces. When I had done them, I saw other possibilities in composing that way, and it led me on.

*JVZ: Today when I listen to them, they have an experimental, exploratory quality, and even though they are made from the same material, they each have their individual characteristics. Perhaps the Fugue is the one that sounds the most "traditional."*

AG: Well it is. As you know, I am not particularly interested in style. When I am composing, as I was with these three pieces, I am interested in what the Germans would call the "Problematik," what the implications are in a particular kind of material and a particular idea. I suppose that you could define the idea of writing from white to black and black to white in two parts as a kind of polymodality, as one voice remains the same and the other one gradually involves more chromatic pitches. How one combines them is a matter for the composer. If someone else decided to do the same, their ear would choose different combinations.

*JVZ: Looking at how modes are constructed where you hear the same pitches against a different key note in turn, it's similar to what you are doing, but you take it further with an array of shifting relationships in it as you go along. It's experimental harmonic work, and it's almost like you create a catalog of modal relationships.*

AG: I think the idea of chromatic notes gradually being introduced wasn't invented by me, it had just been ignored by me. When composers are writing in a panchromatic serial manner, they are hardly concerned with that aspect of music. Listeners of more traditional music are quite accustomed, when listening to Chopin, Brahms, or Schubert particularly, to hear the enharmonic move, and they are used to regarding modulation as a real emotional shift. This was the first time in my life that I concerned myself with that sort of thinking, because I normally didn't give a damn for all that!

*JVZ: Did you find when you were writing these works that you "felt" the music differently?*

AG: I not only felt differently, but I heard differently. I found that when I had done the exercises I derived from the C.P.E. Bach book, my ear had changed. I don't pride myself for having a marvelous ear. I never have had one and I know many people who have much finer ones than I do, but I found I was much more conscious of the role of the bass note than I had been before. There was a slight shift in the way I perceived music, because I suspect that even when I played and listened to Romantic or nineteenth-century tonal music, that I had ignored the role of the bass notes; the bass was merely the bottom part. But then, it's like I suddenly heard the bass!

*JVZ: I want to bring you back to something you said to me many years ago, how the way the* Fugue on the Notes of Psalm 4 *came out was a surprise to you, and if you had thought about it beforehand, you might not have done it.*

AG: Well, I never know how my pieces are going to turn out when I start them, and if I had, I might not have been able to write any of them. I think it was Roger Sessions who wrote that you can have an idea and it's like you are saying before you compose that "I am going to write a blue piece, or a green piece" (I think Mozart described the same thing in one of his letters). You have a very precise idea of what you are going to write, but it's important to get rid of that idea and have faith, because composing always demands a certain act of faith. The technical apparatus that you choose has something to do with your original idea. What it has to do with it, I don't know, and I have never known. All I know is that I believe when I go for a walk and I think of something, it seems to be a finished piece, like in a dream. I think the Mozart letter refers to it as being like a dream and only the time element is missing; and composing is filling in the time element. But in the meantime, as we all know, dreams vanish, and you have to take it on trust that what you are doing, combining elements and adding things up, has something to do with that original dream.

Richard Hall once said to me, rather interestingly, that he thought that you kept the front of your mind busy with calculations, numbers, rows, adding and subtracting, counterpoint, and all the other things that composers do, in order that the back of the mind, the subconscious, or the "superconscious" as some people would describe it, has a free rein; it can go where it wants. I think that's more like a metaphor than anything, but it is a description of what you're doing, of this relationship to an original idea.

Now the circumstance of the writing of the Op. 38a *Psalm 4* was that there was certainly some kind of preliminary idea, but then I forgot it. Otherwise I wouldn't have written a piece of fifteen minutes instead of the two or three minutes that was required!

*JVZ: When you are in the middle of composing a piece, you follow where it leads you.*

AG: And you have to go there!

*JVZ: I took it that this is what you meant when you made that remark to me many years ago about the* Fugue on Psalm 4, *and also that in a way you were looking at it, listening to it, and thinking, "Well, now I have done that and I have a feel for it, what am I going to do?" because there were implications there for moving forward. Would that be fair?*

AG: Looking back on it at the time, audiences were shocked by these pieces. People like to put composers in their appropriate drawers in the cupboard, and these pieces weren't from my drawer! And so commentators tried to explain this. First of all, some said I was going conservative because I had just obtained a prestigious appointment to an ancient university (Cambridge). Or, that I was reaching middle age and that I was more prepared to compromise than when I was younger. All sorts of things were said, which may all be true as far as I know, but none of this occurred to me because I was concerned with the doing of it. I know I have my vanity like everybody else and would like to be loved as a composer, but that's not what it's about.

*JVZ: Speaking for me at the time, as your young student who was used to your serial music, I heard them as being unexplainably mysterious. I didn't understand them. I will say the first time I heard the* Psalm 4 Fugue, *I loved it. I never thought one could write a piece like that in our era. However, when I think about it now, almost fifty years later, it makes total sense to me how it could have come out of you.*

AG: Well the *Fugue* is meant to make sense. It's rather a simple piece. You were talking about modality, and of course now we look back at modality not as it originally existed, but at the characteristics of modality when it has been revived. And it has been revived in a number of different ways. For instance, you could say that Mussorgsky found a lot of his characteristic harmonies and melodic formulas by having grown up with Russian church music, which is very likely. And you could say that Catholics who still have the benefit of knowing the service of the mass before the reforms, and who were brought up with Gregorian chant, would be affected by it in a reasonable way. So you might say that Debussy carried a certain feeling for modality, and you could certainly say that Stravinsky did.

As I told you, the first thing Richard Hall did when I became his student was to make me write pieces entirely with the pentatonic scale. He showed me how I could derive harmonies from it. A pentatonic scale is characterized by having no sorts of dissonances, it only has consonances. But if you take a pentatonic mode, and you write it out as a scale, then like you do with the tonal scale, you take notes 1, 2, 3, 4, 5, and below 1 you put 3, and below 2 you put 4, etc., and it creates harmonies not exactly in the tonal sense, but a form of varied doubling. This was the first way that I began to compose, and in fact, it is the technique I applied to twelve-tone rows a few years later.

I started by taking two pentatonic scales, a white note one and a black note one, i.e., D-F-G-A-C, and E-flat-G-flat-A-flat-B-flat-D-flat, and using both, that gave me ten notes. What I would do later didn't occur to me at the time, I just juxtaposed them. I invented a bit in one of the scales and a sort of consequent with the other. When I came to composing with twelve-tone rows from the time of the *Two Choruses, op. 14*, that I wrote for the John Alldis choir, followed by the *Little Symphony* and so on, I was using a very similar technique. I was creating a redundancy (harmony) by taking one hexachord and adding two following notes below each note in turn (1 with 3 and 5, 2 with 4 and 6, etc.) and doing the same with the second hexachord so that I had six-note structures. This became the basis for several pieces, and from that it developed. Now there were more elaborate things involved than in that rather crude description, but it is essential to show the connection between the original pentatonic composing, and where I was ten years later.

*JVZ: One of the things I learned when trying out your twelve-tone technique in a few of my pieces is that you can have pretty decent overall control of the sound world you occupy by originally constructing your row in such a way that it gives you a particular harmonic/melodic content.*

AG: Exactly, but you can actually overdo it if you aren't careful. You could say that about Messiaen's modes of limited transpositions from his book *Technique of My Musical Language*, which we studied with Richard Hall in Manchester. Almost anybody can create the Messiaen sound by following what he says in the book. I would have said that is not a good thing; it's too simple. But at that time in the 1950s, while on the one hand we were interested—Richard Hall, me, Max Davies, Harry Birtwistle, John Ogdon, and others in the class—in the use of twelve-tone rows, we very rapidly wanted to go away from the characteristic circulation of all twelve notes as in the classical form of the technique. If you look at the structure of Maxwell Davies's first piece, his trumpet sonata, he is using the square of twelve-times-twelve rows, but then not using any rows but going across diagonally in a systematic way. There was one note, then there were two, three, etc. That's how he constructed it. It's a purely mechanical system, but it led him on to his later technique of magic squares, which I rather regret he got caught up in too much.

At that time, we were interested in all the composers who were using artificial modes, not Dorian or Lydian, but modes that were derived from hexachords. In Josef Rufer's interesting book, *Composition with Twelve Notes Related Only to One Another*, he explores the idea of developing modes, and as I mentioned before, in *The Lamentations of Jeremiah* by Krenek, you find that he was using twelve-tone rows divided into hexachords which he made to resemble modes. (Whether it was entirely successful or not is up to the listener to decide.) You could say that about Babbitt with his combinatorial hexachords and semi-combinatorial hexachords which were originally made public in an article he published in *The Score*, a journal in the 1950s. His technique had a strong effect on me and I used it consistently until *Psalm 4*.

We had this preoccupation because our musical culture wasn't Schoenbergian, it was much more Hindemithian—music for ordinary people. Richard Hall had written twelve-tone pieces for recorders, or similar instruments that had a range of a few notes, and he combined modes derived from twelve-tone rows. This came about during the general strikes in Britain in the 1920s, when he had written music for the striking miners to play.

This was a sort of idea that many composers had at the time—not Webern, not Berg, but Eisler, certainly, and many other pupils of Schoenberg—that somehow this technique and new way of thinking could be generalized into a musical language. There were many ways of doing it, but the way that particularly appealed to me, and still appeals to me, is the notion of a modality that could be derived from a hexachord.

You invent a row, say an all interval one, then you divide it into two halves of six notes each and then you arrange the hexachords in scales and you get something that is analogous to a real mode. (I don't know why they had to be two sets of six notes; you could divide them into 7 and 5, or 2 and 10, etc.)

*JVZ: I can see why you do that, as it is natural to seek some kind of symmetry.*

AG: Yes.

*JVZ: In relation to talking about modality, you wrote in your book* Finding the Key *about Messiaen's class:*

> *Having talked about the basis of music in nature, he turned to human music. First came rhythm and accent—Greek and Hindu rhythms, irrational values—then ancient and exotic modes (again Greek and Hindu) and pentatonicism. There followed the ethnic study of music: antiquity and exoticism; world folklore; South America, China, Japan, Mongolia and Korea; Hungarian and Russian folksong; and finally Gregorian chant, which remarkably enough, came under the same heading.*

*Was this kind of study in Messiaen's class all modal study?*

AG: Yes, it was. It sounds very glorious the way I wrote it, but in fact it was much more vague. It depended on a series of books of folk songs from all over the world that were harmonized with tonal harmony in a completely inauthentic way, but that Messiaen thought were striking. That's all that was available then. Now we would regard them as laughable. Messiaen was a pure musician. He knew things as sounds and had no theory that added up to anything. Nowadays we have a much more profound knowledge of the world's ethnic music.

For instance, take Messiaen's "Indian" rhythms. He had never heard any Indian music because there was none to be heard in Europe at that time. The culture of raga came to Europe from India for the first time in the 1950s, and it was only vaguely understood. Messiaen got his information from the Conservatoire's *Encyclopedia*, where, if you looked up "Indian modes", you would find all of Messiaen's modes. And they didn't come from common practice in India, but were out of medieval treatises, which also looked at possible combinatorial rhythms made out of different values. It was the same with Greek rhythms, and of course Greek poetry in Homer's time was written with limited numbers of iambic strophes, dactyls, etc. Messiaen was interested in more complex things that were abstract formulations, patterns of symmetry, etc., which I don't think anyone had ever used; they were purely speculative.

*JVZ: What about his synesthesia? He frequently associated sounds with colors, tastes, and smells, etc.*

AG: It was completely genuine with him. I felt at the time I was studying with him that on the one hand I was aware I was with a great man, probably the last indisputable genius composer, but on the other hand, he was very naive, like Henri "The Douanier" Rousseau. He liked bright colors and imitation forest scenes, like Disney. And there wasn't so much difference between Disney and Rousseau except that Rousseau was a different sort of genius than Disney. Messiaen at the time was, to my ear, entering the period of his most interesting pieces. *Turangalila* was finished and in the past and he was under the influence of Boulez, composing *L'Oiseaux exotiques*, *Chronochromie*, and *Livre d'orgue*, my favorite Messiaen pieces.

The mentality was one that I couldn't understand because I didn't have the same relationship to sound that he had. Which is why he was a great composer and perhaps I am not, because maybe a great composer should relate to sound.

*JVZ: I love the same pieces you do, and I have listened to Messiaen since my student days and adore his music, but I still don't understand how he made it. Perhaps there was a certain misunderstanding of cultural information from other places, like India and so forth, but you can hardly discount the implications of these influences—whatever he might have thought that a raga was, or Indian music, or what birds were singing. There was still something in them, whether misinterpreted or not, that ended up inspiring him in creating those incredible pieces. In a way it is authentically original, employing no system or anything like it.*

AG: Yes, it was completely authentic. How he composed, I don't know. Did he improvise on his modes? I think he must have. For instance, if you take the movement of *Chronochromie* with all the strings in many subdivided parts (the one that Stravinsky imitated, though he didn't say so, in his late *Variations for Orchestra*), it can't be random harmony, because it sounds very much in order, and yet very complex. But no one can solve how it was done.

*JVZ: I recently went to a performance in Los Angeles outside at Disney Hall of all thirteen movements of* Catalogue d'oiseaux, *each one played by a different pianist. It was a lot to take in and hard going at times, but there was a kind of uniformity to the sound world. It's not like it was randomly constructed, but it was deeply felt and heard by him in some way. It deepens the mystery for me: where did that music come from?*

AG: There is a dichotomy in all composition. Certain people, certainly ones who are more like theorists, they believe that one employs rows, modes, or something. My father used to say that twelve-tone music would only arrive when composers weren't using rows anymore. People have believed that I set up my pieces with modes, etc., but I am much more inconsistent than that and have always composed more intuitively and freely. By the same token, I am sure that there is no way of telling which part of Messiaen is constructed and which part is improvised. He was, after all, a great improviser. He improvised at the organ every Sunday at the *Trinité*, and he could do such incredible things. You can't differentiate somebody's use of a technique and their free improvisatory character. It's the same in jazz, surely; you can't pull the two apart. And maybe there is more construction in some composers and less in others, but there has to be a balance of the two, otherwise you might write the same piece twice!

*JVZ: What your father said makes sense to me. It's kind of the place we have moved on to now. Panchromaticism is pretty much an acceptable way of creating music now, without having to employ some kind of system or structure as you would have had to do once upon a time.*

AG: Sure. Every film composer can do it. If you look at someone like Leonard Rosenman, the composer who scored the James Dean films *East of Eden* and *Rebel Without a Cause*, he was a very good composer who could do music like Berg without resorting to rows. He could just do it. (I visited him In Los Angeles once and he was a very nice and interesting man.) I have never seen his scores, but hearing the music in the films, it led me to believe that no Hollywood composer had to write out tone rows to make that kind of music!

*JVZ: Well, I always say that film composers are not composing music but musical effect, and you use whatever means necessary to achieve a particular musical effect, whether it's a row of twelve tones or a Dorian modal scale.*

AG: And that's the difference between an employed composer and an unemployed one! An artist is not one who just makes effects.

*JVZ: For me it's very interesting working in both worlds and being able to do one or the other. It's a guilty pleasure to be able to do something without having to think about it so much. Maybe the place we have moved to now, as your father was saying, was inevitable, and maybe nobody saw it coming.*

AG: I think Schoenberg saw it coming. Schoenberg died at the age of seventy-six, but suppose he had lived another twenty years. What would he have done? He would have surely stopped using rows. In fact, he already had. If you look at the *Ode to Napoleon*, and the *Survivor from Warsaw*, there is already a much broader approach to composition than there had been in the *Variations for Orchestra*.

Or an even more interesting speculation: Scriabin died at the age of forty-five after he had invented a kind of harmonic technique with his own chords. If he had lived to a normal old age, such as eighty, what would have become of him? He would have had to go on. And history does go on, and it even gets to minimalism!

*JVZ: The thing about Schoenberg is that he had already been in that other world before. As a young composer, he had different qualities in his music as a result of his education. It's not such a stretch for me to think that he might have ended up doing something in the way you suggest. But Scriabin was, at this particular place, a real mystery: where would he have gone with it? I also think about Webern, who could have easily lived into the 1960s or 70s. What would he have done? Where was he going to go from where he was in 1945?*

AG: One thing I can guarantee is that he would not have become popular if he had lived!

I remember that Webern's pupil Leopold Spinner—a very interesting man and refugee from Germany who worked at Boosey and Hawkes in London—told me he felt that Webern had actually invented a language that was complete in itself, and which you could compose in. But I don't believe that. Things change. After Bach, there was a type of minimalism, and it was that minimalism that developed into the classical age, not Bach. There's a moral in that!

## 13. FIGURED BASS AND IMPROVISATION

*JVZ: We were talking in the last chapter about the Op. 38 triptych. Listening back now to the pieces just before them—*Metamorphosis/Dance, *Third String Quartet, Piano Concerto,* Lyric Pieces—*and the music you wrote immediately after Op. 38 that follows their lead, they have a consistency and are more closely connected than I would have thought. This is especially the case given the different technical approaches between the twelve-tone works and the ones after Op 38, which were made with a different technique and aesthetic, one that incorporated tonality and modality from pre-twelve-tone days. How is it that it seems that way, or am I wrong about the sonic connection?*

AG: As we discussed in the last chapter, during that time around Op. 38, I was self critical because of the use of models. The Third String Quartet had a clear model in Beethoven's Op. 90, *Metamorphosis/Dance* was based on Beethoven's Op. 111, and the Piano Concerto on movements by Beethoven and Mozart. By modeling, I mean I was taking ideas, bar structures, durations, and harmony from them and modeling fairly closely to them, though I was composing dodecaphonic music. I was so self-conscious about doing it too much because I was able to predict what each piece was going to sound like. Some of those pieces just before *Psalm 4* have done very well and received several performances, such as *Metamorphosis/Dance*. Still, I felt uneasy about it, and I was ready for something new.

*JVZ How did you happen upon the way you began to use harmony in the Op. 38 and subsequent pieces?*

AG As I have said, meeting the Bach scholar Ulrich Siegele, whose work was mainly aimed at composers, and learning of his discoveries in Bach's music, opened my eyes to things that were new to me. We also talked a lot about Monteverdi, and the origins of my opera *Arianna* stem from that time. And, of course, my explorations inspired by the C.P.E. Bach book that I have mentioned.

The result of my writing my own exercises from the C.P.E. Bach book was, first of all, the building of an awareness of bass structure, which I had previously ignored. As far as I was concerned, there was no bass in dodecaphonic music—it was just the bottom part! I made up these exercises in the spirit of C.P.E. Bach, which have to do with reharmonization. Given a top soprano part and a bass part, his exercises consisted of various ways of changing the color of the harmony. I gradually started doing my own exercises using these ideas, and in the structure of *Psalm 4* you hear the result for the first time in my music. There are two parts, the first one with two halves, the Gregorian chant the first half, and the second half harmonization of the chant with the organ and viola, i.e., the second commentary each time, that is a reworking of those exercises. That's how I did it.

For the first time I was regarding harmonization as color. If you take the chord of A major, and you put A at the bottom and A at the top, you could put the C-sharp and E in the middle voices, or you could change to C natural and have an A minor chord, or add a B or G, or introduce passing notes into the harmony—rather like Messiaen does as appoggiaturas or suspensions—and you will get a wide variety of colors. It also changes the nature of the melody. It is basically an improvisatory technique that comes out of accompanying singers in the C.P.E. Bach method from the standard practice of Baroque continuo playing on the harpsichord.

*JVZ: C.P.E. Bach was talking about the color of harmony in his treatise, and I was reading through Rameau's harmony book and he says something similar.*

AG: Yes, but Rameau depends on the concept of fundamental bass, which Bach was against. In C.P.E. Bach there is no fundamental bass, there is only composed bass, and it can be anything. If you are interested in this subject, there is a famous article by J.S. Bach's pupil Johan Kirnberger in which he applies Rameau's theories to a Bach fugue from *The Well Tempered Clavier*, and found that there is no way that Bach could have composed in that particular way. If you look at *The Art of the Fugue*, you find that there is no fundamental bass at all. It's not based on Rameau. It is based on an improvisatory technique where you compose a bass line and then recolor the harmony.

*JVZ: One question I had from looking at Rameau obviously related to what you are saying about the relationship of the fundamental to the bass note itself: Was it a practical consideration from his point of view, or was it perceptual—a way of explaining how a listener might have expectations harmonically, and those expectations are based on the fact that even though the bass note is not playing the fundamental, the fundamental is still there in some way, whether heard or not?*

AG: Except that it wasn't! As far as it affected me, it means that you could improvise a bass part and a top part that could be equal, and reharmonize them in a free and improvisatory way. As I had been a bad student and my work on Bach chorales was poor, I didn't then understand the principle, though I studied it quite carefully. It was only when I found out via the C.P.E. Bach book that I understood how when an identical chorale tune is reused by J.S. Bach in his music—for instance in *St. Matthew Passion*—he reharmonizes it, which makes it into something very different. If you look at the Bach chorale book and compare the different harmonizations of the same tune, you can see what I mean. This is what inspired the

Op. 38 pieces, and when I had done that, I had crossed the Rubicon. I couldn't go back.

*JVZ: You have explained that you transferred the idea of figured bass from Baroque to modern usage via the exercises of C.P.E. Bach, and that was the primary process that you went through to reach a new way of composing. Can you explain how that works in your music?*

AG: Figured bass was used by many composers over a long period of time, Ravel being the most recent that I know of. Forgetting about Bach and that period of music, but thinking about what I was doing, if you arbitrarily invent a chord, say, take the first chord from my work *Colossus or Panic*, you'll find that it is a kind of dominant with a lot of altered notes. Following on from Messiaen's idea, I used both the altered notes and the notes from which they were altered at the same time. Explaining it in the simplest way, if you take the chord A-C-E, and you change the C to a D so it is A-D-E, then it is figured 4/5 (like a suspended 4th chord). If you have 3/4/5 simultaneously, you have a variant of the dominant. If you then add the 7, A-C-D-G, and change the D to D-sharp, you start getting a range of harmonies and colors that are all are variants of dominants. And that is the first chord of *Colossus or Panic*.

*JVZ: In a way you are using this harmonic material that is spread out over the scale, taking it out of the realm of what is known as "tonality," the Ionian mode, and putting it in a different place, sometimes combining both the new and old worlds of this material.*

AG: Yes, but I didn't know that was what I was doing. Others have thought they have found one thing or another in this music, like the octatonic scale *à la* Messiaen, Stravinsky, and

Bartók, or that it was a combination of modes, but in fact, it was nothing of the sort. It was improvised. If it had elements of octatonic or modal construction, as the earlier music had—we talked about the influence of Richard Hall at that time and the use of the pentatonic scale—then I was deliberately using tone rows.

One of the important things about my music from that period is that there was never a piece of paper with a series or mode; I invented it directly in sound. And if you improvise, you improvise colors.

*JVZ: And tone, hue, and color in a musical sense, that's what it sounds like to me.*

AG: That's what it is. The only limitation to that is that once I had written out the first idea, then my Schoenbergian background would come back in. Like Helen Carter said about her husband, Elliott, "You can take certain things for granted in Elliott's music." Applying that to myself, it's clear that the experience of dodecaphonic composing and my particular way of deriving it from Boulez, Babbitt, and others obviously affected the way I treated these musical ideas once I had them. It's not that the pieces are improvised for twenty minutes from beginning to end. The original idea is improvised, but afterwards I am treating them as if they were the result of row procedures.

*JVZ: A lot of people, knowing your earlier music and just coming to this later music, would think that there was a predetermined reason for your notes to be in a particular place, but that gets away from the whole concept of figured bass, which is an improvisatory system.*

AG: Yes. Famously at one point of Boulez's life, he felt that he should reintroduce the element of improvisation back into music after total serialism, which was at an end. There was an article by him, which affected me deeply at the time, called "To the Limits of Fruitful Land," quoting the title of a painting by Paul Klee. In that article, he proposed (Boulez always "proposed" before he "did") that improvisation should be reintroduced into music. In order to show how this might be done, he gave examples from Webern's Second Cantata, where there is a redundancy of pitch classes from the row, and Webern improvises. You will find this in the fifth movement of the work. There are other examples too. Boulez did it, but because he used so much material from his row structures and *bloc sonore*, the improvisation just sounds like decoration. I went much further than that.

JVZ: *It is a different way of composing. I know that if I start improvising a piece, I get to the point where I think there is enough material there and I can use what I now have to continue composing through a piece. I think that people who don't improvise in a composition are missing out on an element that makes it more fun. And, even better, this kind of composing often results in a happy accident, something interesting that arises which had not been foreseen.*

AG: Quite right. It introduces the concept of "accident," which is a good thing. Boulez believed that if you have something that happens that you haven't planned or calculated, i.e., an accident, for instance the famous common chord in Stockhausen's *Kontrapunkte* where in writing the notes enharmonically he didn't realize that he had an A-minor chord, then censorship should be applied to it. Or you should alter it in some way (in the tessitura, etc) as to make it so you can't hear it. I believe the exact opposite. If chance, for instance, produces a reminiscence of something from the past, it's like a gift from the Almighty, and has to be retained. I was influenced in this by the painter

Francis Bacon who told me that if a drip falls on his canvas, he could easily remove it but he doesn't. He regards it as part of the painting and works from it.

I felt after a time that the accident—and by accident I mean the chance meeting of durations, pitch levels, and timbres, which either reminisce or fall out of the unity of the idea—was something you should retain, and it should transform the whole piece. I don't know if I ever succeeded in doing it, but that was the idea.

*JVZ: Well you can't ignore it once it's there!*

AG: Yes. It goes towards a kind of anti-method. I was talking with a friend in Jerusalem a lot about Paul Feyerabend's book *Against Method*, which is a quasi-philosophical look at science getting away from the "unique" method. Being slightly anarchistic myself, I was always critical of the too-literal interpretations of the twelve-tone technique, not unlike the way Feyerabend looked at science. I think Schoenberg himself would have also ultimately felt that way.

*JVZ: I know this is jumping ahead a little, but because I was listening to* Arianna, *where you recomposed the lost opera of Monteverdi's, it seems to me that opera has a foot in both worlds—the Baroque and the modern—and you revel in that, which I know is on purpose! You kept the* Lamento *which was all that still existed from Monteverdi's version. Is it the same as the original?*

AG: Not that much the same. It had to be there as I couldn't leave it out. I told you the origins of this from Siegele's remark about Monteverdi. Well twenty-five years later, I decided to attempt it because the surviving libretto was so good, and I wouldn't have attempted it with any other composer but Monteverdi. I composed the scenes in the manner of Palestrina, which I could do very quickly, and each scene took four or five days, seven at most, to write. It was done like strict counterpoint. There is only one factor that I added, and that's one that came from the *Psalm 4* pieces, the idea of introducing flats and sharps, making "black" notes from "white" ones, and making different expressions like we spoke about in the Modality chapter.

In allowing that element, I used the text to suggest more expressive/less expressive, black/white. If you look at the lament, you'll see it is a classical example of that technique because Arianna gets angry, then she says it's not right to get angry and she goes flat again. When I had done my "Palestrina thing" with the sharps and flats setting of the scene from *Arianna*, I then recomposed it according to the harmonic principles I just explained. One of the paradoxes is, in the *Lamento*, the fishermen are listening to Arianna while she is on the beach trying to kill herself. We don't know what they sang in the original Monteverdi because the text exists but the music is missing. I wrote that music so my lament doesn't sound much like Monteverdi because the harmony is changed, and above all, the tessitura is changed, but not so far that you wouldn't recognize the piece. However, the fishermen, on the other hand, sound like Monteverdi, but I wrote that!

*JVZ: There is a perceptual thing I notice about it. At the beginning I think it sounds like Monteverdi, but moving on to the second and subsequent scenes, it sounds more and more like Goehr! A lot of it has to do with the colors of the instrumentation, harmony, etc., but nonetheless, there is still the sound of Monteverdi in it.*

AG: One of the concepts that is very important when you are referring to other music, which is also very important as a compositional principle, is the concept of transparence. It is described in Wollheim's book *Painting as an Art*, when Picasso imitates Goya or Velázquez, or Manet imitates earlier paintings. You have to see/hear the model and your version of it at the same time. It's in the "quivering" of these two things that the distance between 1995 and 1600 is perceptible. The two have to quiver in some kind of temporary dissonance; it has to be audible. If they aren't audible, it's like Max Davies's imitations of Monteverdi's *Vespers* in his *Sinfonia*: if he didn't tell you he was imitating Monteverdi, you would never have guessed it.

*JVZ: Does that mean that any time you are going through the process of composing anything like* Arianna, *you are consciously thinking about this "quivering" aspect (which I find very interesting)?*

AG: Yes, though it's not as simple as that because it's playful, and sometimes in *Arianna* it's a very close parody of Monteverdi, and sometimes it's not. It's a dialogue which is inherent in the structure of all my music.

*JVZ: Yes, I see that. The other thing I notice is that when you are doing a parody of Monteverdi—instrumentally, trombones and percussion sound etc—you really hear it as Monteverdi. But then you sneak in the colors of the vibraphone, guitar and harp, and it becomes kind of a floating or flowing sound, like Boulez's* Le Marteau sans maître *in a way.*

AG: Yes, your remark about *Le Marteau* is exactly to the point, because that is the kind of thing that I was deliberately doing.

*JVZ: And to me that is "quivering," but on a textural, pure sound level, not a compositional level.*

AG: That's absolutely right. But you see, *Le Marteau* is *Le Marteau* all the way through, whereas my piece is only sporadically *Le Marteau*!

*JVZ: Sometimes it's just there in the background and you can almost imagine that Monteverdi had these instruments.*

AG: Well, of course, I chose the instruments deliberately to try and create a bogus Monteverdi orchestra.

*JVZ: And that really works. But to me, it's the kind of ensemble that you would choose for one of your pieces anyway! One of the things I know about you is that you often leave things out if you don't need them, like "I don't need cellos or double basses in this orchestra so I won't use them." And for a lot of composers that would mean asking themselves, "How the hell am I going to be able to do this piece without a cello or a double bass?" But leaving the cello out, that's as important as putting in the vibraphone.*

AG: Absolutely correct. In the nineteenth and early twentieth centuries, orchestras got bigger and bigger. That type of 1910 enormous orchestral piece, quite apart from being able to get anyone to perform it, I view with considerable distaste. I think the essence of instrumentation is that by leaving instruments out, you make other players do things. For instance, I use the double bass very high, but I wouldn't do that if I had a cello in my ensemble. But it's not a cello, it's a double bass! I have done that all my life.

*JVZ: There is a practical aspect of it too, when you make a conscious choice to do these kinds of things. I have never really thought about what I can do without. I always think, "Oh, I need this." But maybe I really don't need it.*

AG: Well, that's the normal thing to do alright. But being a naturally perverse person I like to leave things out, I like gaps. I like to leave things out in conversation and also in music.

*JVZ: And that gives your music an air of mystery too, but the other thing is the textural aspect of it.*

AG: Yes, it's "jumping."

*JVZ: There is a kind of "vibration" or "quivering" in this music because of that!*

AG: Yes. Incidentally, the first piece where I made a sort of Monteverdi orchestra is in *The Death of Moses, op. 53*. And because I liked the way it worked in that piece, I dared do it for the *Arianna* orchestra.

*JVZ: Well,* The Death of Moses *is also an exploratory piece in my view, including the ensemble that you used.*

AG: That piece was also another approach to music theater, because it's meant to be performed with people moving around on the stage or platform. It's not terribly dramatic in an operatic sense, but the singers move around to various positions.

*JVZ: And you also like the saxophone!*

AG: Yes. That came about when my clarinetist colleague Alan Hacker thought he might be able to do for the sax what he had done for the clarinet, so I wrote an alto sax part for him in my music theatre piece *Shadowplay, op. 30*.

I like the saxophone very much and did a lot of research and listening until I felt I could write for it. Thanks to my friend Gunther Schuller, I listened to a lot of great jazz saxophone performers, like Eric Dolphy and John Coltrane, and learned a great deal. Harry Birtwistle pointed out to me the advantages of the soprano sax over the others, so I used soprano saxes in pairs to stand for Baroque cornetti in *Arianna* and *The Death of Moses,* and they are almost indistinguishable in sound from the period instruments.

*JVZ: A happy accident, you might call it!*

AG: Indeed!

## 14. WORDS INTO MUSIC

*JVZ: One subject that comes up again and again with composition students is how to select texts for setting to music and how to approach composing with them. I know this was a big topic while I was studying with Goehr in the 1970s, and he gave me some very good advice on the matter which I have followed ever since, and which I pass on to my students. We get to that and much more in this chapter. He has extensive experience in composing with a wide variety of texts—from Shakespeare and Byron to Confucius and Kafka—in many different forms of vocal music: opera, cantata, oratorio, songs, music theater, choral, and even a dramatic solo piece. He has a lot to say on the subject that would be of use to young composers as well as music scholars.*

JVZ: *How do you go about selecting texts, and can you distinguish the differences between dramatic, choral, and song texts?*

AG: Picasso said, "I do not look for, I find," and I agree with that. I don't usually go looking for texts, but things strike me. The texts that I've chosen have almost always struck me because they have something to do with me; I recognize in them, even if they are from a long time ago, something that connects with me.

I have always read poetry and drama, and attended the theater. My Opus 1, unfortunately lost, was a song cycle based on *Hebrew Melodies* by Byron. They were poems which are glosses on songs, and I went on from there.

JVZ: *You have an extensive list of compositions employing texts from throughout your life. Have the texts you have used, or your thinking on how to set them, changed in any way since you were younger?*

AG: It changes every time I set a text. The poets I dealt with at first were English: Blake, with whom I identified strongly because I was very sympathetic to his sort of political anarchist views; Milton, and Shakespeare. Then in 1959, I bought *Gleanings in Buddha-Fields*, a book by Lafcadio Hearn which had little Japanese Buddhist poems. On the train from York, where I was at the time, to London, I composed adaptations I made from the book as *Four Songs from the Japanese, op. 9*, and that was the beginning of my interest in Asian poetry, especially Japanese and Chinese. So there are two distinct strains of interest.

A third strain is German poetry, which came through my friendship with the late Austrian poet Erich Fried, who lived in London. He was the BBC's commentator to East Germany, whom I first met at the time of composing my first opera, *Arden Must Die (Arden muss sterben)*, for which he wrote the libretto. I then set some of his poetry to music in a song cycle, *Warngedichte, op. 22*. The song texts were *und Vietnam und*, from his collection *Einundvierzig Gedichte*, which were short poems about euphemisms used by the military during the Vietnam War.

JVZ: *Where did the idea of* Arden Must Die *come from, and how did you develop the project with Erich Fried?*

AG: The *Arden Must Die* text is from a semi-apocryphal play, *Arden of Faversham*, noteworthy because one or two scenes were allegedly by Shakespeare, and the rest by someone else. It's not a great play, but it follows the lead of *A Yorkshire Tragedy* from 1608, which was the first play that dealt not with noble or mythological themes, but with everyday life. The original reason why I decided on this text was that I heard the play on the radio and it struck me as being a bit like a Janáček libretto. Janáček was new to me at that time, and I was very enthusiastic about him. He wasn't really new, but he was new to London, brought there by Charles Mackerras, who in fact conducted the first performance of my *Arden*. The preface of the published edition of the play calls *Arden of Faversham* "Lady Macbeth of the Fields," referring to the story by Nikolai Leskov, "Lady Macbeth of the Mtsensk District," made famous by the Shostakovich opera.

I then took it to Fried, who I was introduced to by Georg Eisler, the painter son of Hanns Eisler. He agreed to do it and what he did was miles away from the original inspiration. The play had to be rewritten as an opera. The fashionable playwright of that time, after the success of his *Marat/Sade* play in London, was the German Peter Weiss. Fried, I think, took his model from Weiss or from Brecht. The original is partly in iambic verse and partly in prose, and not very distinguished, and Fried recast it into little rhyming verses. He made one of the characters into a witness called Mrs. Bradshaw from an original character called Bradshaw in the play. Mrs. Bradshaw, a big contralto part, was rather like the characters played by Margaret Dumont in the Marx Brothers' films, who was always shocked by what she saw, but never did anything about it.

The setting of these little rhyming stanzas presented an enormous difficulty to me, as I had never done anything like it before. I had to take note of the metrics of the original, because they were so upfront, and sustain what were essentially rhyming couplets for two hours. How do you do that? A composer who was new to me at the time was Charles Ives. I took a device from him in order to vary the metric of the word setting. A basic theme of the opera is that here were a lot of people telling untruths. Wherever there was a lie, I separated the orchestra accompaniment and the voice part, so that the voice perpetually sang its strong accents on the wrong beat. So if you say we're writing in 3/4, where you get strong beats on the first beat and weak beat on the second and a semi-strong beat on the upbeat, I put the strong one on the second or even sometimes on the second quaver of the second beat, so that they would actually have to sing a 3/4 in the wrong parts of the bar.

This device, which I adapted from Ives originally, can also be found in music by Michael Tippett, who took from English madrigal writing a kind of polyrhythmic technique of the kind you find in pieces by Orlando Gibbons. In fact, Gibbons figures in *Arden* in the one scene that takes place in London—an attempted murder in a marketplace—and I used Gibbons's street cries in that particular scene. The Gibbons English madrigal style was adapted by Britten and Tippett—Britten with great care and Tippett very boldly—into a kind of polyrhythmic structure. And that is where, probably, you find 3/4 bars beginning on the wrong beat, or 3/4 against 2/4 simultaneously, or 5/8.

Such was the rhythmic complexity in the score that in Hamburg the orchestra had very great difficulty in playing it. Mackerras, the conductor, found a bar that was in 5/8 which only had one beat in it, and then next to it a bar in 2/4 which had five beats in it. He thought that was an example of the sort of idiocy or difficulty, whichever way you look at it, of the setting. It is very complex, but I had to do it that way in order to make the difference between lies and the truth sound natural. And in that sense, my feeling about word setting is conventional.

The best English word settings in our time were by Britten. They are very well done, though they're not often what you expect. He realized the metrics and the rhythm of the words very carefully, and to great effect, as did Tippett. I very much like Tippett's tendency to use melismata—long extended collections of notes on a single syllable—as he did, for instance, in the song cycle *Boyhood's End*, on a text by

W.H. Hudson. It's very rich verbally. And so I derived my models from English music, rather than from Schoenberg and Webern, whom I didn't find so interesting from the point of view of word setting.

JVZ: *I know that you have set a lot of Shakespeare, and the influence of the language of Shakespeare, as well as Milton and Blake, in text settings in your work, and in the work of other English composers such as Britten and Tippett, is very apparent. Would I be right in saying that there is a strong musical attraction to the rhythm and mellifluence of the spoken language itself that can be almost overpowering at times?*

AG: It can be. I have to say that not everybody who has performed my vocal music has been in accord with the way I've done it. The most notorious critic of it was John Eliot Gardiner, who did the first performance of my cantata *The Death of Moses*, op. 52. He considered my vocal setting quite perverse in that strong syllables were on weak beats, as usual creating the rhythmic polyphony I go in for. But there is another aspect of this that enters into it. Normally when I set words I make them my own by repeatedly speaking them. I speak them again and again and use the result in my settings.

I've often quoted the story of Prokofiev during the making of Eisenstein's film *Alexander Nevsky*, which he was writing the score for. Eisenstein says he repeatedly played the rushes of a scene to Prokofiev, and after a while, Prokofiev started beating time with his hand. Eisenstein asked him what he was doing, and Prokofiev said: "Well, when I've got a speed, the tempo, and the rhythm of the scene, then writing it is no trouble." The same is true for me in word setting. I repeat the words again and again, and I speak it idiosyncratically, as everybody else does. It's not just the King's English in its generalized way. It spews out of one's culture and what one is and where one comes from, and all the rest. So it's very possible that I read these poems or words that I set incorrectly from someone else's point of view. And having repeatedly read them I start beating time or walking them so that I get the speed, because the speed of the words determines the texture of the music.

For instance, if you have very few beats in a line: "We're talking now about words," you could say it: We're talking (1) now (2) about words. Or you could say: (1) We're talking now about words (2). The difference is that version one would be quavers against crotchets, whereas version two would be more like a recitative with semiquavers against one long beat. Now that determines the way the vocal line, pitch level, and the shape of the line are going to be set, as well as their relationship to the accompaniment. And that's always what I've done. I do it in instrumental music too, incidentally.

JVZ: *You just reminded me of the advice you gave me that I mentioned at the beginning. The first time I brought you a piece of mine with a vocal setting, you had a look at it and said, "No, no, no, you are noodling about too much. Just read the poem!" So I read you the poem (it was in Spanish), and you said, "There you go. That's much better. It doesn't sound anything at all like what you have written." And you basically told me what you just said here. "Read your poem, feel the tempo of it, then write down the rhythms as you spoke them, and there is your piece." You said that I would say it differently from anyone else, but that's the way I felt the poem and that's the way I have to use it. That's what makes it mine. Ever since that day in 1977, I have done it the same way and it always works. It is certainly one of the most valuable (of many!) pieces of advice I have ever gotten from you as a teacher and I pass it on to my students in the very same way.*

AG: The point is, the way you feel a poem and then the way you speak it will differ from person to person. People come from different backgrounds, and they would read it differently, and therefore they should set it differently. Incidentally, I tried to explain this to a group of six Chinese students in Beijing many years ago. I took a Chinese poem, and I showed them how I would set it in English. And when we discussed it, they said, "We're looking for a way of writing music in China which isn't just a copy of whatever is current in Europe, but is our own thing." And I said, "Well, you should start with the language." So after pontificating to them on that subject, they pointed out to me that written Chinese was the same everywhere, but, of course, the spoken versions in Mandarin, Cantonese, and other dialects were completely different languages. However, the principle is still the same.

I often wondered about the rhythmic structure of my friend Max Davies's music, and I've often found the way he wrote things down very perverse indeed. And then I realized that when he spoke he had a very mannered way of speaking, i.e. not at the same speed, but suddenly faster, rather jerky, and then fast and slow. And that's exactly how he composed it. So I think there's a strong case to be made that if you want to understand how people write words, listen to how they talk.

JVZ: *I strongly believe that there is, or should be, a relationship between the way composers and actors work. Like them, we find emotional authenticity by feeling our way through the words and what they are expressing. And we have to draw on our own experiences to do that. Do you do that yourself in some way?*

AG: Yes, surely. Of course, you have to make the texts your own somehow. Any magpie can settle on any book and pick out some words it likes. But you've got to make the words your own. I can tell you a funny story in relation to this. When T.S. Eliot died, a theatrical performance was organized, and lots of famous actors and other people, including painters and sculptors, participated to memorialize the great poet. One of the participants was Laurence Olivier, who read from the *Four Quartets*. Olivier was a great actor and orator, and when he spoke he left great pauses in between words which weren't grammatically or syntactically sanctioned. I mean, he put them in, because that's the way he felt it. And following him, the next person up to read was Groucho Marx who read from *Old Possum's Book of Practical Cats*. Groucho, who was a friend of Eliot's, started reading, and he left unnaturally long pauses in places in the sentence so it wasn't like verse at all. When he finished, there was a long pause, and then he said "my interpolation," commenting on Olivier. That's a very dramatic and comic example of the way in which someone in one case distorts a text which they read, and in another case, distorts it creatively because they each make it their own.

I worked in the theater myself for a while, and the relationship between the director and the actor struck me as interesting, in the respect we are talking about, when the actor would speak some lines—whatever the play was—and the director would stop the actor and say, "Do you think: 'I feel the meaning of a particular line?'" (And we're talking about meaning, not just rhythmic structure.) "Perhaps the meaning would convey something more if you were to leave out a little emphasis, or make a little emphasis here not there: 'We're talking about setting *text*,' setting the words idiomatically, or 'We're *talking* about setting text.' You see, you can change the meaning of something, by the emphasis and by the choice of accent." And when the director spoke like this to the actor, I noticed the actor silently listening for a bit, absorbing what the director had said, and then he would say "Thank you." And then he would go back, and he would do it slightly differently. Not necessarily the way the director had suggested, but he'd absorbed the director's point. And in a way, setting to music is rather like that too—obviously in opera, but equally in song.

When performing Schumann's *Dichterliebe* or Schubert's *Winterreise*, great singers bring these works to life in that way. It's not just the dots on paper that they're singing accurately, but they have to bring the words to life; they must live!

JVZ: *What about the context of your settings? Does poetic imagery in any way dictate the way you compose the music around the words?*

AG: Yes and no. I don't do it in the way that composers in the past have done it, such as Schubert or Britten; something like "rivers bubbled" that led to semiquaver passages. And there is certainly a repertoire of imagery in poetry which has been realized in various ways by many composers, Schubert and Schumann particularly. However, in the tradition I come from, the more Brahms/Schoenberg one, that type of musical imagery is not very strong. The cliché imagery that exists in a great deal of songwriting, I tend to avoid—not so much now as I did when I was younger, when I quite specifically didn't want to use the geography, history, or psychology to be found in the imagery as a lever. That would be getting too near reduplication, something like what they call "Mickey Mousing" in Hollywood film music. (However, with very good film music, even if you don't look at the screen, you can very often disentangle the story simply by listening to the music.)

Hanns Eisler set a great deal of Brecht, whom he was very close to. I was once with Eisler in the BBC studios during a rehearsal of one of his Brecht collaborations that uses a remarkable poem called *Potsdam unter den Eichen* (*Potsdam beneath the oak trees*). It's a poem about a procession of the First World War in which marchers are carrying banners saying "To Every Warrior His Home"—but their home was death and they were all dead. The poem relates that in each coffin was a man, or a bit of a man like his arm, leg, or head, and the banner of the German flag was ironical. The vocalist singing it was full of passion in trying to express these words. Eisler walked up to him, smiled and said, "Sing it like Schubert, because it's bad enough as a text without your actually multiplying or augmenting the effect of the words. If there's a dialectical opposition between the words and the music, it makes a stronger effect."

Now that's something which I very much believe in, too. I have consciously tried to contradict imagery in order to create a kind of dialectic, not only in *Arden*, which is my most Brechtian piece, but in all sorts of later pieces. I don't underline because that strikes me as—in all but the best pieces—a bit jejune and simplistic, and I don't like that. In a sense, you always have to ask yourself, especially when you're dealing with a very prominent poet such as Milton, Shakespeare, or Rilke, whether what you're doing is necessary; because, after all, these are great poems in their own right, and what justification do you have for adding something to them. The only justification is that you're saying something from your point of view now, which slightly alters it. You have to do a bit more than "do no harm." You actually have to do some good, or you've got to try anyway.

JVZ: *What are your first considerations of a text? Do you think about how it flows as music? Do you hear a tune in a particular line or poem? Or is all that discovered through a process of composing?*

AG: I don't know that there's one answer. I think it varies. If it's a poem, say a Shakespeare sonnet, as I described earlier, I find the meter, the speed/tempo, and through finding those elements I discover the relationship between whatever is going to accompany the sung lines of the poem, whether it's other voices, a piano, or instruments. If I've solved all that or at least gotten some inkling of what it should be, then

I find the notes, and there aren't so many that it can *be*! For instance, whether you try to set the words to a melody—which may have many or few notes but is in itself complete—or whether you set them to a kind of recitative which has repeated notes, these are matters that arise out of the initial tempo and metric considerations. Of course there is also the business of the upbeat, the strong beats, and the weak beats. Shakespeare and a lot of English poetry by and large is written in iambics, and if you stick too closely to the text, it makes it rather dull rhythmically. But you can vary it, as indeed Shakespeare does continually, by enjambments and by variations within the iambics. You can either realize these so you don't notice them, or you can "imply" from your own speech and add something different to it. A poet I admire greatly, Gerard Manley Hopkins, also composed music, and he uses rhythmic complexities, silences, and very difficult things I'd never think of setting because it's already music. And there are certain poets I wouldn't set. I'd never set Paul Celan, or others very rarely, like Rilke, whom I have set only once. These are poets where the music is already so embedded in their poems that you could only compose it by reduplicating it, and reduplication is exactly what it's *not* about.

JVZ: *If you are setting great poets whose works are often read, or in the case of Shakespeare spoken in the context of a play, do you take any cues from the way actors speak their lines, rhythmically or otherwise? For instance, there is a great deal of variation in the way Shakespeare's words are brought to life by different actors, but mostly they tend to float over the iambic pentameter which is only tacitly apparent as a background structure.*

AG: In terms of iambic settings in Shakespeare, the greatest actors flow over the top of it, and you would notice it, but you wouldn't actually hear it when they speak. You shouldn't notice it, because it would lead to a "Baa Baa Black Sheep"-type of reading. Nevertheless, the metric underpinning has to be somewhere. It's a sort of psychological perception. For instance, nowadays in England at least, I think, the speaking of verse or drama has declined because actors mainly earn their living through television. And television very rarely realizes meaning, but imposes a kind of style on top of it. We've talked elsewhere about style and meaning, and you should not put a style on it. However, much of what you hear now is simply stylized speech that doesn't actually convey the meaning of the words at all. If you look at Laurence Olivier's film of *Henry V* from 1944, you can understand every word; whereas, if you hear Shakespeare acted by present-day actors, very often you can't understand what they're saying.

JVZ: *How do you go about structuring a setting? Do you "feel" your way through it?*

AG: I don't know really. It seems like in all compositions, what I write in the morning seems to dictate the continuation later. When I was younger I made plans that I would write out. Churchill famously wrote sentences and phrases on little cards, and then he'd structure them into a text. Emulating that sort of thing when I was younger, I would write out the text. I never compose off a printed text, I always write it out myself by hand, and I learn something by doing that. I used to shape the piece visually on the paper, with big and small letters, and lines which were to be emphasized, but it has been some years or decades since I've actually done that. I used to be much more structurally conscious, whereas now, in a sense, I do it by instinct. It should have flow, and it also should have interruptions. Sometimes I'm negligent of interruptions and add them later, because I think when you take a reasonably short text, if you don't interrupt it, nobody is going to listen because they will get bored with it. Also few audience members can hear the words anyway, unless they read along in the program notes.

When I was growing up and my father took me to an opera, he would make me read the libretto first or I wasn't allowed to go. There's no way one can assume that the audience have the least idea what the words are about unless they prepare themselves. Of course if you look at Ira Gershwin or any other lyricist in the American popular song tradition where there is great vocal setting, the words were often written after the tunes. That would be a very good way of doing it. In great song composers such as Gershwin or Cole Porter, it's certainly the case that you can hear the words because the words were written to the music, which came written first. Probably some part of that goes back to very ancient times. Ezra Pound of course believed that words and music were initially one and the same. He believed that there was a unity—as there is in Dowland—between the writing of the words and the composing of the music, that it was all one thing, and they then became separated over the centuries. The American popular song composers, Gershwin, Porter, Richard Rodgers, etc., tried to put them together again, and did so very successfully.

JVZ: *It's typical for composers to work very closely with a librettist in composing an opera, but we rarely do it for other types of vocal projects. Interestingly, you created a text using poems and fragments by many poets in collaboration with the literary critic Frank Kermode in your* Sing, Ariel, op. 51, *for three sopranos and five instrumentalists. That is a unique way of working in my experience. How did that partnership come about and how did it work?*

AG: Frank Kermode, who was a good friend and a great man, originally thought I was just asking him for an anthology of his favorite poems. I explained to him that I can choose my own poems and I didn't need him to recommend any (although I'd be interested in what he suggested). But what I really wanted him to do was to "compose" a text, and that's what he did. He was a poet when he was very young, but he didn't continue writing poetry and became a literary critic and philosopher instead. What he wrote for me is something called (from Italian) a "cento," a poem made of other poems. And that's a very one-off thing; you can't do that every day. It would take a particular empathy between collaborators to do that, and not everyone would want to because most poets would want to write their own poems. There is not one line in *Sing, Ariel* which is by Frank Kermode. On the other hand, if you look at the text as a whole, none of the cento text is explained by its constituent parts. It's all quotations. However, if you read the text by itself without my setting, it also reads like a poem, and it's quite unique from that point of view. Britten used various texts in his *Serenade* for tenor, horn and strings, and in his *Spring Symphony*, but Britten is the unity, and the words are clearly by several poets. My *Sing, Ariel* is something quite different, and, offhand, I can't think of anything like it.

JVZ: *You have said many things in this discussion that would be helpful to young composers who want to set texts. If you could draw on your extensive experience in working with words and boil it all down to one sentence of practical advice to students, what would it be?*

AG: They should read the words out loud while they clap their hands to get the tempo, and that's their piece. That's the one thing which I would strongly advise any composer working with a text to do.

## CODA
## MY FATHER'S SON

*Walter Goehr conducting. Goehr Archive*

## 15. WALTER GOEHR

AG: Looking back, I have noticed that the influence of teachers and mentors on me occurred almost at once, even if it took me a long time to realise and absorb it. This is not the case with what I took and still take from my father. He died young at the age of fifty-seven in 1960 (when I was twenty-eight). But, for as long as I can remember, and though our relationship was emotionally changeable, if not actually contradictory, it went on and still goes on.

On the piano in our home, he had left a copy of Stravinsky's *Serenade in A*. I was fifteen or sixteen at the time. Poor pianist that I was (both my parents were accomplished players), I tried to make out the *Hymne*, which is the first movement of it. My father came into the room, having heard the jungle of wrong notes, and said to me, rather sharply, "You can't possibly either play or understand this piece." Fair enough. But then he added, "Such a piece is part of a continuing tradition of which you know nothing and which I am not able (or don't want) to explain to you."

Why do I still remember this as if it was yesterday? Probably I have always seen my father's remark as vaguely aggressive and part of his rejection, early on, of any musical aspirations I had at the time, but which I surely would not have talked about with him. Now I am not so sure. It all depends on what he, and later I, meant by the word "tradition."

The term has a vaguely conservative resonance to it. Certainly, you wouldn't see any connection between people who described themselves as "traditionalist" and those who thoughts of themselves as radical innovators. But wouldn't Arnold Schoenberg, my father's teacher and an unseen but continuous presence in our house, have described himself with both those terms?

Today, a traditionalist, in music at least, is one who prefers to play or listen to the repertoire, often rejecting anything that is outside the Bach to Brahms period. My father was certainly not one such. First and foremost, he was a modernist, but his interests went in all directions: Purcell, Monteverdi, rare and unknown Schubert, Mahler, Stravinsky, and Bizet, to name but a few. What, then, did he mean by "tradition," which he could not or would not explain? In so far as I include him here as mentor as much as a father, everything I observed about his musical activities, as much as anything he told me, qualifies that role.

Tradition is craft and technique. It is learned by imitating, by accepting criticism and improving, and is at best an apprenticeship. This would be true for any music, not only Western, but Indian, Chinese, and African. Had my father meant only that, he could easily have explained it, or sent me to a teacher. But there's something else: European musical culture, from Machaut on, has a changing quality which is hardly observable in any other, or if it is we can hardly have ever been aware of it.

The apparent dichotomy between craft-technique and the changing quality of different types of music at different times and in different places may have been what my father could not explain to me.

My father's life had extended from his time in Berlin when, at the age of eighteen, he had conducted operetta, to his final times with Bach's *B Minor Mass* and Monteverdi's *Poppea*. He also created and performed the first radio opera, *Malpopita*, in 1931. As a composer in Germany he wrote a symphony, and in England, he wrote music for the weekly wartime feature "Marching On," scored a few films, including David Lean's *Great Expectations*, and much else.

Without doubt, the formative influence on his musical life was the time of his study with Schoenberg. He regarded

Schoenberg as the pre-eminent composer of his time, but he felt that only the most gifted could follow in his footsteps and he did not count himself among them. When composers, performers, and critics, not to mention audiences, failed to take up Schoenberg's work—particularly that using twelve-tone rows—he did not see this as casting any kind of shadow on him, but felt, instead, that the music and techniques were beyond the grasp and even understanding of the majority.

When as a student in Manchester I became enthusiastic for the ideas and compositions of Schoenberg (that was the time of his earliest collection of essays under the title *Style and Idea*), I thought of them not as a forbidden Olympus, but actually as an aid to learning to compose. The note rows, at first twice the pentatonic scales (white and black notes), but soon all twelve, helped me with aural identification of what I wrote and gave me the feeling of having taken a step forward. At the same time I became interested in passacaglia, ostinato and variation form, all allied to Schoenbergian preoccupations.

My father blew hot and cold at all this. More than anything he hated pretentiousness of any kind. He did not allow me to have a corduroy jacket, because it smacked of pseudo-artistic posing. He was after all a highly able and well-trained composer, distinguished in his ability to write good harmony, able to do fugue, and a master of newer orchestration. (In fact, it's a footnote to the history of music in England, that with his pre–Second World War Orchestre Raymonde of fifteen or so first-class musicians, he introduced the now common chamber ensemble to this country, and made all the arrangements for them, from Handel to Duke Ellington.) On the strength of this, he was appointed by the BBC to do the music for all the war-propaganda programmes beamed to occupied Europe and the "operas of the news," "Marching On," for home consumption. So it was perhaps only natural that he should look with puzzlement and suspicion at a son who was adopting what he thought was beyond him as a kind of prop to learning. As an all-rounder in Germany while learning the works of his teacher, he veered closer to the *neue Sachlichkeit* of Hindemith and Kurt Weill. In England it was mainly his incidental music for radio, film, and theater that showed the influence of Ravel and Debussy as much as anything else.

Certainly, he regarded my limited abilities as a kind of snobbery brought on by my English public school education, a kind of refusal to dirty my hands with ordinary money-earning work. On the other hand, he became interested in what I was doing and in my friends in Manchester; first, my teacher, Richard Hall, and then my fellow students Peter Maxwell Davies, Harrison Birtwistle, and John Ogdon.

My father was himself an inspirational teacher. For some years he had a regular conducting class that I sometime sat in on. It did not, as far as I could tell, concern itself with conducting as such, but rather with repertoire. It consisted of the close reading of a selected score, not according to any theoretic or systematic point of view, but with attention to anything that struck the eye or ear. First of all, appropriately for aspiring conductors, there was phrase-structure. This was detailed by observation of texture, polyphony, and instrumental color, metric placing of the phrase, and its elaboration and decoration. The significant role of individual notes at the cadence or at the beginning of a phrase was of particular interest to him. It is particularly apparent in the attention paid to Schoenberg's *Erwartung*, which forms the most important part of the study of Schoenberg's approach to the twelve-tone technique. I wrote an account of my father's ideas in the essay "Arnold Schoenberg's Development Towards the Twelve-Tone System" in my book *Finding the Key*.

Such an *undoctrinaire* approach to the study of repertoire—not unobservant of the writing of Schoenberg, Rudolph Réti, and Heinrich Schenker, as well as Hugo Reimann—affected me greatly. I never experienced such deep reading elsewhere, and I have tried to do it myself and establish it in the syllabus of any institution I was associated with. Of course, it is not a method or school of analysis; quite the contrary. It will be done differently by different people. The essential of it is a kind of collective slow-motion of a composition, in as much detail as can be brought to bear on it.

Michael Tippett liked to say that the best way for young composers to learn was to attend rehearsals. Being a conductor's son, I was particularly lucky to be dumped in a corner of, first, BBC radio broadcasts, and later, orchestral rehearsals at Maida Vale or Camden High Street Studios. My father, who suffered from the cold, appeared in a pilot's helmet and a number of pullovers and cardigans which he shed throughout the session. He talked a great deal and conveyed his wishes by grunts and other descriptive noises. Unlike Boulez, who expressed his dislike for Schoenberg's thick harmonies in the bass, and Brahms and Reger, I remember my father shouting, "Dirtier! Dirtier like me!" about a chord.

I think he "pushed" the music more than, say, Sir Adrian Boult. This even characterized his Monteverdi performances, which were much brighter than those of others at later times. (With the exception of John Eliot Gardiner's, who has a somewhat similar taste for color.) Of course that was before the existence of authentic instruments. Sometimes, as I grew older, I followed with a score, but that's not necessary. At a rehearsal, you hear the selected fragment repeated and altered a tiny bit. Performances are for the whole piece, rehearsals for details.

My father's attitude to my compositions varied from total negation, with or without abuse, to comparative enthusiasm. Certainly, the negative was painful, but it overlaps the role of mentor, or rather overshadows it, with father-son matters, which do not concern us here. He did not necessarily criticise me in so many words, but I knew when he thought what I had written was pretentious or just plain rubbish. On the other hand, despite himself, after an outpouring of verbal abuse, he could get interested enough in a piece to start recomposing it. I particularly remember that one (and only) occasion when he became really interested in my Piano Sonata, op. 2, and recast the middle slow section built on an ostinato, transposing, reharmonizing, and going well beyond anything I had been able to imagine. That's the version in which the piece was played and published.

Certainly, I learned a great deal from this. Rewriting became a constant preoccupation and it remains so up to the present. But I had to stop myself taking up a piece once it had been finished. ("Put a double bar on it!" said Richard Hall.) One of the difficulties, or hazards, of improving a passage is that it wipes away what was originally imagined and written down. If an already finished piece is rewritten, very often the original idea, its atmosphere, and its intention are simply forgotten. Of course, this does not apply to details heard in performances which can be improved. But this is a real Scylla and Charybdis: you have to sail down the middle and tie yourself to the text. I suspect my father veered on the side of endless possibilities. This may be part of the reason why he never composed concert pieces once he came to England. At the end of his life, he took out unfinished fragments which he had written decades earlier, and he even suggested that we collaborate somehow. However, it was never discussed how this might be done, and nothing came of it. I even remember that he wanted us to write an opera on Baron Corvo's novel *Hadrian the Seventh*, but if this sounds as if on a positive note, that would be overstating things. The good moments were matched by negative and discouraging—probably correct, but exaggerated—criticisms. When I began to get paid commissions, he was amazed, "You mean they actually give you money to write this stuff?" He had always told me, "By all means do what interests you passionately, but do something practical to make a living." But finally, to end on a good note, in 1959 he conducted the premiere of my cantata *The Deluge, op. 7*, and it was very well received.

I said that I was separating my father as a mentor from my father as a father. I now see that this is a false distinction. He could only be one thing to me and I one thing to him. I could never have received what I received if he had not been my father and he couldn't or wouldn't have given what he gave had I been anyone else. This makes me think of fathers and offspring who shared the same profession, like Carl Phillipe Emmanuel and Johann Sebastian Bach, and the Mozarts, Kleibers, and Serkins.

I frequently discussed this with Oliver Knussen (who managed to pass away on the same date as his own father). We decided that as a consequence of the father-son relationship, there were certain things which we could not do. But to compensate, there were other things which we could take for granted, that others had to learn—if they could.

In fact, a father, by example, admonition, and rare praise, transfers what little he knows and the thing my father said he could not tell me: some bit of the tradition. That is what one receives in a verbally sometimes ill-defined way from a teacher and mentor.

# STUDENT MEMORIES OF GOEHR
## AS TEACHER AND MENTOR

I first met Sandy in late 1964, when I had been "passed" to him by Peter Racine Fricker with whom I had just started studying. Fricker had been offered and accepted a post in California, so it was good of him to take the trouble to look after my interests in that way. As things turned out, his aid proved to be a life-enhancing as well as life-changing act. My first impression of Sandy was tempered by a sense of awe, though he instantly made me feel not only welcome, but also someone worth paying attention to. His studio was a room jam-packed with musical scores (many if not most from his father's collection), a large grand piano, a desk, and two chairs. The rest of the house clamored with the voices of his children interacting with their mother, Audrey.

Having newly graduated from studies in physics, and already being an interested and practicing visual artist, I may have been unique in the type of young composer he was teaching at that time. It may have been my cross-disciplinary horizons that shaped the way our working together unfolded. I'd like to say straight away that Sandy never sought to teach me how to compose. What he did do, however, was to provide me with technical advice, on form especially, but much more importantly, introduce me to bodies of reading and research as well as to experiences, which confirmed that he understood that my stance on musical composition was open to many forms of analogy and fusion.

It was Sandy who introduced me to the writings of Klee, Kandinsky, Goethe, and Ruskin, figures who, in one way or many, have had a seminal influence on my work and thinking. In fact, I must describe Sandy as the embodiment of the perfect primer for an imagination in need of focus and stability. There was never a question of following in his "pathways," though of course the music of the Second Viennese School formed an integral part of his open-ended discourses. He left one in no doubt about the music that attracted or repelled him. In addition, there was no holding back from the philosophical domains that were continuing to engage him with musical ideas, some of which found their ways into his superb chamber theatre pieces.

I don't think I fully understood what a humanist and humanism were at that time, but Sandy is one of the most splendidly humane persons

I have ever known. This fabulous generosity of spirit filters through every part of his music, his writings, and his teachings. Fortunately for me, it also spills into a friendship that has ebbed and flowed for more than fifty years. I think his perspectives on teaching are so diverse and yet intense that, for a composer like me, I have never stopped feeling that Sandy continues to profoundly affect the way I approach composition. I once thought he would disapprove of the way my music has unfolded—it seeming to be so much less rigorous than his own—but he has always encouraged me to follow my own pathways and I owe almost everything to him in giving me multiple signposts to aid my journey.

Freud may have had it that we end up hating our fathers. There have been times when I have doubted Sandy's influences on me—denied them even. However, today I freely acknowledge and celebrate what he has shared, and continues to share with me. And I'm not ashamed to say that the decades of my studentship with him have been threaded through with admiration and love.

Edward Cowie

My studies with Sandy began in September 1958 while I was still a student at Morley College, London. He took over Iain Hamilton's orchestration class, and immediately opened my mind to the correct way of approaching not only orchestration but also composition. Within a year he had agreed to take me on as a private composition student, and from then on I was able to set aside my years of careful academic groundwork and think creatively, almost without inhibition. He did not try to influence me technically—for instance, although we discussed serialism a lot, it was not a requirement. However, he did influence my approach to compositional *thought*, so his outlining of serialism in a non-Darmstadt manner simply fed its way into my technical vocabulary as a nutrient to my own steadily developing technical language.

A further very rich nutrient was provided in the sequence of revelatory analysis seminars that Sandy regularly held at his home, to which I was invited along with several other composers at a comparable stage of development. We studied the classics, and one or two twentieth-century works, in huge detail, thereby revealing significant below-the-surface logic. This *subtle* approach to logic has formed my approach to composition ever since—not simply imitating the classical greats, but translating those modes of thought into my own personal musical idiom. That was the other huge importance of Sandy's influence: that he never tried to model one's idiom, style, or technique, only the way to use them most effectively, and, I stress, clearly. And at last, the relevance of those years of studying harmony and counterpoint became clear! This thread of thought has run unobtrusively through my composing for sixty years now, as my latest orchestral pieces will show.

Yet another influence has been on my own approach to teaching the discipline. I can't claim to have the same level of insight as Sandy showed me, but approaching my students' works from the same direction as they do helps me give useful and constructive guidance, i.e., following each student's own line of logic, thereby helping, in Sandy's way, to develop it.

Thank you, Sandy, so very, very much!

Anthony Gilbert (1934–2023)

In 1983, I arrived at Cambridge on a Fulbright year to study with Sandy. I was thirty-three, brash and confident, using my overseas time to conclude the non-coursework part of a DMA at Columbia University. In our weekly meetings, Sandy was at first a bit mysterious, speaking in such generalities that I was unsure about what he was trying to tell me. Gradually, as he realized that his observations would need to be more pointed, I came to understand that his method was to get me to focus on all the things I seemed not to have fully considered, or, perhaps, not considered at all. I remember a moment when, trying to feel better about being called out in a precise and devastating way for each of my compositional and conceptual shortcomings, I consoled myself by imagining that if Sandy had been teaching Beethoven, he'd likely have asked him about his lack of Italianate melodic sense. So I started to push back, sticking to my guns as I tried to regain my footing.

The real turning point came when he asked me: "How do you assess the quality of your basic material?" I responded in what I thought a perfectly sensible way. I said that I believed the basic material to be less important than how it was developed. To buttress my argument, I gave two examples from Beethoven: the *Diabelli Variations*, and the scherzo movement of the String Quartet, op. 59, no. 1. Sandy looked at me dismissively and said: "Those are the exceptions." So I tried another tack. I said that lacking an objective way to make such quality assessments, the question was impossible to answer, and so I chose not to ask it. He glared at me and with much intensity in his voice said: "It is the *only* interesting question."

I was stunned to silence. I have no recollection of what followed. I walked around in a fog for a few days. After I regained my composure and was able to compose again, I started to open myself up more fully to Sandy's comments and my music began to change for the better. I am still trying to answer this question. Of course it can never be answered definitively, even in the most personal of ways, but Sandy was right. It *is* the only interesting question, and, I'd add, the most crucial one as well.

David Froom (1951–2022)

In the early 1980s, Sandy Goehr, as one of the first Western music "diplomats," came to China to give master classes to introduce twentieth-century music at both Beijing Central Conservatory and Shanghai Conservatory after China's thirty years of isolation from the West. I was a composition student at the Shanghai Conservatory then. Sandy was an enlightener who, within his short stay in Shanghai, imbued our avid students with the most modernistic compositional techniques and numerous repertoires that we had never heard of.

Later in my life, in 1993, I was selected as a composition fellow for the Tanglewood Music Festival. It was very lucky that Sandy was the composer-in-residence that year and I had the opportunity to study with him on a one-on-one basis for the entire summer. During the Festival, I also had stimulating weekly seminars and discussed various music issues with Sandy and my fellow composers. Sandy's encyclopedic knowledge, natural wit, and warmth deeply influenced me. Under his guidance, I completed my string quartet, *Yang-guan Songs*, which was premiered during the Tanglewood Music Festival Contemporary Week, and it became one of my most successful compositions.

Thank you, Sandy, for being one of my important mentors through my career!

Joan Huang

The treasured time I have spent over the years in conversation with Sandy Goehr is of immense value to me. Not only is Sandy always a huge fountain of wisdom and insight on so many topics, but his constant validation of my writing often provides me with the encouragement I need at just the right moments.

Many of our discussions have started with my despair at a musical problem I thought I was having, but Sandy always has a way of exploring an issue and evaporating even the hint of impasse. Equally helpful are the times when he challenges me to defend or clarify something I was actually quite confident about. The immediacy of his questioning always gets to the core of the matter and reveals avenues of creative thinking that were not obvious before. Sandy has shown me how to "hold" a musical tradition, or specific idea, but then write freely "away" from it. I found my artistic integrity in discovering how to listen, absorb, and then set something aside in order to get on with my own writing, knowing its essence was living subconsciously in my ears.

Sandy's ability to open up new, fruitful thought processes or compositional possibilities is one of his greatest qualities as a teacher. He is truly exceptional at passing on solutions and practical methods from his own practice and fitting them to very specific areas of discussion. Every single note is, of course, of great importance, but Sandy's readiness for wide-open thinking that isn't restrained to "the march of the bar line" (or how to get from one note to the next) is liberating.

Many of the "tools" that I consistently rely on have come directly from Sandy: his thoughts on how to create and thoroughly make use of short scores or sketches for large-scale structural designs, his concepts from film and theatre, and text setting and timing, to name just a few, have radically enhanced my compositional life and have been a valuable source for teaching myself.

I remain hugely in debt to Sandy for his time and compositional generosity.

Emma-Ruth Richards

Sandy Goehr is uniquely valuable as both composer and teacher. In both capacities he has carefully shunned easy answers. Having encountered early the twin certainties of Communism and total serialism, much sooner than most he came to see both as the dangerous chimeras they were. Nor did he fall into the trap of puerile neo-Romantic fantasies. Right from the *Two Choruses* and the *Little Symphony* and up to the present, Goehr has repeatedly confronted the basic materials of his art with a frankness that recalls Paul Klee's *Pedagogical Sketchbooks*. Like Klee, he has provided puzzlement as well as delight, enchantment going hand in hand with dystopia.

In one area in particular, harmony, a topic on which even today so few composers show any sustained interest, Goehr has addressed the problem of creating a characteristic musical language with courage and determination, even as his music underwent radical changes over more than five decades. But those changes have also taught him the value of uncertainty. No wonder Goehr's endings are so memorably offhand—he has an aversion to the false rhetoric and unreality of a grand conclusion.

As John Hollander's specially written text for Goehr's oratorio *The Death of Moses* concludes bluntly: "I've said what I've said. / That will abide."

And thus, too, Sandy Goehr!

Julian Anderson

I first encountered Sandy Goehr in my teens, not only on Radio 3 but also in a memorable forum led by Hanns Keller in London (possibly at the ICA) around 1966, when I was still in school. Keller was stirring up debate with Maxwell Davies, Birtwistle, and Goehr on the "direction of modern music." When I graduated in 1970, the coincidence that Southampton University was opening a trail-blazing one-year course in contemporary composition with Goehr as its visiting specialist was too exciting to ignore. (The resident team of Jonathan Harvey and Eric Graebner was nothing to sneeze at either.)

Goehr's fortnightly visits and tutorials were conceptually wide ranging. He was by no means bound to Schoenbergian rows. Looking back, I realize he was at a fascinating midlife juncture, thirty-nine, just returned from a year in America, embarking on a second marriage, and on the brink of a stylistic renovation himself. As a teacher, he was staunchly opposed to the doctrinaire tuition he'd encountered under Messiaen. He wanted to get inside the machine. He focused on the seeds of creativity: take a plainsong, reinterpret its notation as a model, and imagine your own style of outcome. I did, and found it opened up an immensely fascinating world. By the time that the opportunity arose to study with Sandy in 1973 at Leeds University, I was winning prizes and had been broadcast on Radio 3, but his insights and suggestions were always helpful: indeed they still are!

At the heart of Goehr's capacious mind lies a mastery of the paradoxical. He said of one former pupil, "my worst pupil. Whatever I suggested, he *did* it!" The creative mind in a nutshell.

Geoffrey Poole

I met Sandy Goehr at Yale during the period 1969–71 when I was in his graduate music theory class. He engaged in creative explorations and seemed to have somewhat iconoclastic tendencies that I liked very much. While revealing to us interesting details of Messiaen's theoretical approaches, along with comments on other contemporary trends, Sandy seemed disinclined to restrict himself in his own approach. I remember him as decidedly building on his own creative imagination rather than sticking with the tried and questionably true ways.

Goehr took time to explore a world of possibilities as an autodidact, continually refining the depth of his intuitive instincts, forming his own artistic convictions and their variations. He did not seem stuck on one path. He relished possibilities and evolved his own creative ways and means. In essence, Sandy is an inspiration as an individual idiosyncratic artistic explorer.

I remember that he was quite personable and invited his graduate students to his home to share conversations, wine, and a crackling fireplace. He encouraged a cordial intellectual, humanistic, thoughtful, creative ambience that was casual and quite communicative with sparks of intensity, enthusiasm, and mind play. In sum, Sandy Goehr was a role model teacher by being who he is: authentic. I am grateful for his influence.

Daria Semegen

## BIBLIOGRAPHY

### SELECTED BOOKS AND WRITINGS BY AND ABOUT ALEXANDER GOEHR

Goehr, Alexander, *Finding the Key: Selected Writings* (Faber, 1998)

Goehr, Alexander, "Learning to Compose" in *Alexander Goehr, "Fings ain't wot they used t'be"* (Akademie der Künste Archiv Berlin, 2012)

Griffiths, Paul, *New Sounds, New Personalities: British Composers of the 1980s* (Faber, 1985)

Griffiths, Paul, "'…es ist nicht wie es war…': The Music of Alexander Goehr" in Alexander Goehr *"Fings ain't wot they used t'be"* (Academie der Künste Archiv Berlin, 2012)

Grünzweig, Werner, "In Dialogue with the Past" in Alexander *Goehr, "Fings ain't wot they used t'be"* (Academie der Künste Archiv Berlin, 2012)

Hall, Michael, *Music Theatre in Britain, 1960–1975* (Boydell, 2015)

Latham, Alison, ed., *Sing Ariel: Essays and Thoughts for Alexander Goehr's Seventieth Birthday* (Ashgate, 2003)

Northcott, Bayan, ed., *The Music of Alexander Goehr: Interviews and Articles* (Schott & Co, 1980)

Rupprecht, Philip, *British Musical Modernism: The Manchester Group and Their Contemporaries* (Cambridge University Press, 2017)

### BOOKS AND WRITINGS MENTIONED IN THE TEXT

Bartolozzi, Bruno, *New Sounds for Woodwind,* second edition (Oxford University Press, 1982)

Benitez, Vincent, *Olivier Messiaen, A Research and Information Guide* (Routledge, 2007)

Feyerabend, Paul, *Against Method* (New Left Books, 1975)

Goehr, Laelia, photographs, *Musicians in Camera*, text by John Amis, foreword by Yehudi Menuhin (Bloomsbury, 1987)

Herrigel, Eugen, *Zen in the Art of Archery*, with an introduction by D.T. Suzuki, translated by R.F.C. Hull (Vintage, 1999)

Mann, Thomas, *Die Entstehung des Doktor Faustus: Roman eines Romanes* (S. Fischer Verlag, Frankfurt am Main 1949), as *The Story of a Novel: The Genesis of Doctor Faustus*, translated by Richard Winston and Clara Winston (Alfred Knopf, New York 1961).

Messiaen, Olivier, *Technique de mon langage musical* ("Technique of my Musical Language", Alphonse Leduc, Paris 1944)

Milstein, Silvina, *Arnold Schoenberg: Notes, Sets, Forms,* Music in the Twentieth Century series (series ed. Arnold Whittall), (Cambridge University Press, 1992)

Piscator, Erwin, *The Political Theatre*, translated with chapter introductions and notes by Hugh Rorrison (Eyre Methuen, 1980)

Rosen, Charles, "Influence: Plagiarism and Inspiration" *19th-Century Music* 4, no. 2 (1980): pp. 87–100.

Rufer, Josef, *Composition with Twelve Notes Related Only to One Another*, translated by Humphrey Searle (Rockliff, 1954)

Schoenberg, Arnold, *Fundamentals of Musical Composition*, edited by Gerald Strang and Leonard Stein (Faber, 1967)

Schoenberg, Arnold, *Preliminary Exercises in Counterpoint*, edited and with a foreword by Leonard Stein (Faber, 1963)

Schoenberg, Arnold, *Structural Functions of Harmony*, revised edition with corrections by Leonard Stein (Norton, 1969)

Schoenberg, Arnold, *Style and Idea: Selected Writings*, edited by Leonard Stein and translated by Leo Black (Faber, 1975)

## TV AND RADIO

**Arnold Schoenberg: Bogeyman, Prophet, Guardian**
BBC TV, 1974, presented by Alexander Goehr, Produced by Barry Gavin. Playlist of two episodes in six parts:
https://www.youtube.com/playlist?list=PLFs7AkUbVmp6vKVqBAPdrBymq5aaeyYcv

**The Survival of the Symphony**
BBC Radio 4, The Reith Lectures, 1987
A Series of Six Lectures Presented by Alexander Goehr

1. The Old Warhorse
   https://www.bbc.co.uk/programmes/p00h196j
2. An Orchid in the Field of Technology
   https://www.bbc.co.uk/programmes/p00h194k
3. Past and Present
   https://www.bbc.co.uk/programmes/p00h193q
4. A Licence for Licence
   https://www.bbc.co.uk/programmes/p00h192k
5. Let the People Sing
   https://www.bbc.co.uk/programmes/p00h191k
6. Stand Up and Be Misunderstood
   https://www.bbc.co.uk/programmes/p00h18yf

**GOEHR WORKS LIST**

## STAGE WORKS

| TITLE | OPUS | YEAR | COMMENTS |
|---|---|---|---|
| Arden muss Sterben / Arden Must Die | Op. 21 | 1966 | Opera in two acts |
| Music Theatre Triptych I Naboth's Vineyard | Op. 25 | 1968 | Dramatic Madrigal |
| Music Theatre Triptych II Shadowplay | Op. 30 | 1970 | |
| Music Theatre Triptych III Sonata about Jerusalem | Op. 31 | 1970 | Cantata |
| Behold the Sun – Die Wiedertäufer | Op. 44 | 1981–4 | Opera in three acts |
| Arianna | Op. 58 | 1994–5 | Opera in eight scenes |
| Kantan and Damask Drum (i) Kantan | Op. 67 | 1997–8 | Opera |
| Kantan and Damask Drum (ii) Damask Drum | Op. 67 | 1997–8 | Opera |
| Kantan and Damask Drum (Un)fair Exchange | Op. 67 | 1997–8 | Opera |
| Promised End | Op. 83 | 2008–9 | Opera in 24 preludes |

## INSTRUMENTAL WORKS

| TITLE | OPUS | YEAR | COMMENTS |
|---|---|---|---|
| Fantasia | Op. 4 | 1953–4 rev. 1959 | For orchestra |
| Hecuba's Lament | Op. 12 | 1959–61 | For orchestra |
| Pastorals | Op. 19 | 1965 | For orchestra |
| Symphony in One Movement | Op. 29 | 1969 rev. 1981 | For orchestra |

| TITLE | OPUS | YEAR | COMMENTS |
| --- | --- | --- | --- |
| Metamorphosis/Dance | Op. 36 | 1973–4 | For orchestra |
| Deux Etudes | Op. 43 | 1980–1 | For orchestra |
| Symphony with Chaconne | Op. 48 | 1985–6 | For orchestra |
| Colossos or Panic | Op. 55 | 1991–2 | Symphonic fragment after Goya for orchestra |
| … second musical offering (GFH 2001) <br> (i) Overture with Hendelian Air <br> (ii) Concerto with Double | Op. 71 | 2000–1 | For orchestra |
| Adagio (Autoporträt) | Op. 75 | 2003–4 | For orchestra |
| When Adam Fell / Durch Adams Fall | Op. 89 | 2010–11 | For orchestra |
| Two Sarabands | Op. 98 | 2015–6 | For orchestra |

**CHAMBER ORCHESTRA**

| TITLE | OPUS | YEAR | COMMENTS |
| --- | --- | --- | --- |
| Little Symphony | Op. 15 | 1963 | For small orchestra |
| Sinfonia | Op. 42 | 1979 | For chamber orchestra |
| Still Lands <br> (i) Sumer is Icumen in <br> (ii) Scherzo on Schumann's Freundliche Landschaft <br> (iii) Variations on Schubert's Ins Stille Land | Not listed | 1988–90 | Three pieces for small orchestra |
| Broken Lute | Op. 78 | 2006 | Six pieces for violin |
| Broken Lute | Op. 78a | 2007–8 | For alto flute, oboe, and strings |
| … between the lines / zwischen den Zeilen | Op. 94 | 2013 | Chamber symphony for 11 players |
| Double Chaconne with Gaps | Op. 40 | 2019–20 | For ensemble |

## STRING ORCHESTRA

| TITLE | OPUS | YEAR | COMMENTS |
|---|---|---|---|
| Little Music for Strings | Op. 16 | 1963 | |
| Fugue on the Notes of the Fourth Psalm | Op. 38b | 1976 | For string orchestra |
| Romanza on the Notes of the Fourth Psalm | Op. 38c | 1977 | For two violins and two violas concertante and string orchestra |

## WIND ORCHESTRA

| TITLE | OPUS | YEAR | COMMENTS |
|---|---|---|---|
| Three Pieces from 'Arden Must Die' | Op. 21a | 1967 | For wind band, harp and percussion |

## SOLO INSTRUMENT(S) AND ORCHESTRA

| TITLE | OPUS | YEAR | COMMENTS |
|---|---|---|---|
| Concerto | Op. 13 | 1961-1962 | For violin and orchestra |
| Romanza | Op. 24 | 1968 | For cello and orchestra |
| Konzertstück | Op. 26 | 1969 | For piano and small orchestra |
| Concerto | Op. 33 | 1972 | For piano and orchestra |
| Cambridge Hocket | Op. 57 | 1993 | For four horns and orchestra |
| Schlussgesang | Op. 61 | 1996 | Six pieces for viola and orchestra |
| Marching to Carcassonne | Op. 74a | 2005 | Serenade for piano and chamber orchestra |

## CHAMBER MUSIC

| TITLE | OPUS | YEAR | COMMENTS |
|---|---|---|---|
| Sonata | Op. 2 | 1951–2 | For piano |
| Fantasias | Op. 3 | 1954 | For clarinet in A and piano |
| Capriccio | Op. 6 | 1957 | For piano |
| Variations | Op. 8 | 1959 | For flute and piano |
| Three Pieces | Op. 18 | 1964 | For piano |
| Nonomiya | Op. 27 | 1969 | For piano |
| Paraphrase on the dramatic madrigal 'Il Combattimento d Tancredi e Clorinda' by Monteverdi | Op. 28 | 1978 | For solo clarinet |
| Prelude and Fugue | Op. 39 | 1978 | For three clarinets |
| Chaconne for Organ | Op. 34a | 1979 | A transcription of Chaconne for Wind |
| Sonata | Op. 45 | 1984 | For cello and piano |
| … in real time | Op. 50 | 1988–91 | Cycle of pieces for solo piano |
| Sur terre, en l'air | Op. 64 | 1997 | Three pieces for viola and piano |
| Suite | Op. 70 | 2000 | For violin and piano |
| Symmetry Disorders Reach | Op. 73 | 2002 | For solo piano |
| Ariel, Sing | Not listed | 2003 | For solo flute |
| Composition of A's and G's | Not listed | 2004 | For solo soprano saxophone |
| Fantasie | Op. 77 | 2005 | For cello and piano |
| Broken Lute | Op. 78 | 2006 | For solo violin |
| Almost a Fugue | Not listed | 2007 | For two pianos |
| manere | Op. 81 | 2008 | Duo for clarinet and violin |

| TITLE | OPUS | YEAR | COMMENTS |
|---|---|---|---|
| Hymn to Night | Op. 87 | 2010 | For viola with piano accompaniment |
| Variations | Op. 93 | 2012 | For solo piano |
| Seven Impromptus | Op. 96 | 2014 | For two pianos |
| manere II | Op. 81b | 2016 | For clarinet and violin |
| manere III | Op. 81c | 2016 | For clarinet and horn |
| Sonatine | Op. 106 | 2020 | For solo piano |
| Four Pieces | Op. 107 | 2021 | For violin and viola |
| Surrounding Silences | Op. 108 | 2022 | For solo piano |

## THREE TO FIVE INSTRUMENTS

| TITLE | OPUS | YEAR | COMMENTS |
|---|---|---|---|
| String Quartet No. 1 | Op. 5 | 1956–7 rev. 1988 | |
| Piano Trio | Op. 20 | 1966 | |
| String Quartet No. 2 | Op. 23 | 1967 | |
| String Quartet No. 3 | Op. 37 | 1975–6 | |
| String Quartet No. 4 "In Memoriam John Ogdon" | Op. 52 | 1990 | |
| Quintet "Five Objects Darkly" | Op. 62 | 1996 | For bass clarinet, hn, vln, vla, piano |
| Double Duo | Op. 66 | 1998 | Duo for violin and two violas |
| Piano Quintet | Op. 69 | 2000 | |
| … around Stravinsky | Op. 72 | 2002 | For violin and wind quartet |
| Duos | Op. 95 | 2006–13 | For two violins |
| Quintet for clarinet and strings | Op. 79 | 2007 | |
| Since Brass, nor Stone | Op. 80 | 2008 | Fantasy for string quartet and percussion |

| TITLE | OPUS | YEAR | COMMENTS |
|---|---|---|---|
| Largo Siciliano | Op. 91 | 2012 | Trio for horn, violin, piano |
| After 'The Waking' | Op. 101 | 2016–17 | For wind quintet |
| Piano Trio No. 2 | Op. 100 | 2017 | |
| Vision of the Soldier Er | Op. 102 | 2018 | String Quartet No. 5 |
| Waiting | Op. 103 | 2019 | Piano and wind quintet |

## SIX INSTRUMENTS OR MORE

| TITLE | OPUS | YEAR | COMMENTS |
|---|---|---|---|
| Suite | Op. 11 | 1961 | For flute, horn, harp, vln/vla, vlc |
| Concerto for Eleven | Op. 32 | 1970 | For chamber ensemble |
| Chaconne for Wind | Op. 34 | 1974 | |
| Lyric Pieces | Op. 35 | 1974 | For wind instruments and double bass |
| … a musical offering (J. S. B. 1985)… | Op. 46 | 1985 | For 14 players |
| Variations on Bach's Sarabande from the English Suite in E Minor | Not listed | 1990 | For wind instruments and timpani |
| Uninterrupted Movement | Op. 59 | 1995 | For solo cello, 4 celli and others |
| Idées fixes | Op. 63 | 1997 | Sonata for 13 |
| "… kein Gedanke, nur ruhiger Schlaf" (in memoriam Olivier Messiaen) | Op. 61a | 1998 | From Sclussgesang Op. 61, arranged by the composer for chamber ensemble |
| 2 notes only for Ollie… | Op. 74 | 2002 | For 11 players |
| Marching to Carcassonne | Op. 74 | 2002 | Serenade for piano and 12 instruments |
| Overture | Op. 82 | 2008 | For ensemble |

## VOCAL MUSIC

| TITLE | OPUS | YEAR | COMMENTS |
|---|---|---|---|
| The Mouse Metamorphosed into a Maid | Op. 54 | 1991 | For unaccompanied voice |
| Four Songs from the Japanese | Op. 9 | 1959 | For mezzo soprano and piano |
| In Thereseinstadt | Not listed | 1962–4 | For mezzo soprano and piano |
| Warngedichte | Op. 22 | 1966–7 | For mezzo soprano and piano |
| Das Gesetz der Quadrille – The Law of the Quadrille | Op. 41 | 1979 | For mezzo soprano and piano |
| Dark Days | Op. 76 | 2004 | For low voice and piano |
| Ulysses' admonition to Achilles | Not listed | 2006 | For baritone and piano |
| Enter King Richard. | Op. 92 | 2012 | For baritone and piano |
| The Deluge | Op. 7 | 1957–8 | Cantata for soprano, contralto, and instrumental ensemble |
| Behold the Sun | Op. 44a | 1981 | Concert aria |
| Sing, Ariel | Op. 51 | 1989–90 | For mezzo soprano, five players and two sopranos |
| Lamento of 'Arianna' | Op. 58a | 1994–5 | For soprano and ensemble |
| Arianna Abbandonata | Op. 58c | 1994–6 | For tenor and guitar |
| Three Songs | Op. 60 | 1996 | For voice, clarinet in A and viola |
| 3 Sonnets and 2 Fantasias | Op. 68 | 2000 | For counter-tenor and viol consort |
| from Shadow of Night | Op. 86 | 2009–10 | For counter-tenor and viol consort |

| TITLE | OPUS | YEAR | COMMENTS |
|---|---|---|---|
| To These Dark Steps / The Fathers Are Watching | Op. 90 | 2011–12 | For tenor, children's choir and ensemble |
| Verschwindendes Wort | Op. 97 | 2014–15 | for mezzo-soprano, tenor and ensemble |
| Combat of Joseph de la Reina and the Devil | Op. 105 | 2019–20 | For 2 soprani, mezzo-soprano, tenor, viola and piano |

## VOICE AND ORCHESTRA

| TITLE | OPUS | YEAR | COMMENTS |
|---|---|---|---|
| Four Songs from the Japanese | Op. 9 | 1959 | For mezzo soprano and orchestra |
| Eve Dreams in Paradise | Op. 49 | 1987–8 | For mezzo soprano, tenor and orchestra |
| TurmMusik/Tower Music | Op. 85 | 2009–10 | For two clarinets, brass and strings with baritone solo |
| The Master Said | Op. 99 | 2016 | For speaker and chamber orchestra |

## CHOIR A CAPPELLA

| TITLE | OPUS | YEAR | COMMENTS |
|---|---|---|---|
| Two Choruses | Op. 14 | 1962 | For mixed a cappella chorus |
| Two Imitations of Baudelaire | Op. 47 | 1985 | For mixed a cappella chorus |
| Carol for St. Steven | Not listed | 1989 | For mixed chorus |
| Cori di Pescatori | Op. 58b | 1994–5 | Four madrigals for five male voices from the opera 'Arianna' |
| Cities and Thrones and Powers | Op. 88 | 2011 | Choral song with keyboard |

## CHOIR AND ENSEMBLE

| TITLE | OPUS | YEAR | COMMENTS |
|---|---|---|---|
| Virtutes | Not listed | 1963 | Cycle of 9 songs and melodramas for speaker, mixed chorus and instruments |
| Five Poems and an Epigram of William Blake | Op. 17 | 1964 | For mixed chorus and trumpet |
| Psalm 4 | Op. 38a | 1976 | For soprano, alto, female chorus, solo viola and organ |
| The Death of Moses | Op. 53 | 1991–2 | For five soloists, chorus, children's choir, and 13 instruments |
| I said, I will take heed (Psalm 39) | Op. 56 | 1992–3 | For double chorus and wind ensemble |
| Broken Psalm | Op. 84 | 2009 | For SATB chorus and organ |
| Babylon the Great Is Fallen | Op. 40 | 1979 | For chorus and orchestra |

## GOEHR DISCOGRAPHY

**Concerto for Orchestra / Little Symphony, Op. 15**
1965, Philips SAL 3497
Goehr – Little Symphony, Op. 15

**Four British Composers**
1965, His Master's Voice ALP 2093
Goehr – Two Choruses, Op. 14

**Songs / Four Songs From The Japanese / Chuench'i**
1967, Nonesuch H-71209
Goehr – Four Songs from the Japanese, Op. 9a

**Modern British Piano Music**
1970, His Master's Voice, ASD 2551
Goehr – Three Pieces, Op. 18

**Goehr – Violin Concerto**
1972, His Master's Voice ASD 2810
Goehr – Violin Concerto, Op. 13

**Alexander Goehr – Orion Trio / Allegri String Quartet – Piano Trio / String Quartet No. 2**
1973, Argo ZRG 748
Goehr – String Quartet No. 2, Op. 23
Goehr – Piano Trio, Op. 20

**Alexander Goehr, Susan Kessler And Roger Vignoles / Lindsay String Quartet – The Law of the Quadrille Is Clear (Songs After Franz Kafka) / String Quartet No 3**
1983, Wergo WER 60093
Goehr – String Quartet No. 3, Op. 37
Goehr – Das Gesetz der Quadrille, Op. 41

**Peter Maxwell Davies / Alexander Goehr – Stephen Pruslin – Piano Sonata / Capriccio / Nonomiÿa**
1983, Auracle Records AUC 1005
Goehr – Capriccio, Op. 6
Goehr – Nonomiÿa, Op. 27

**Alexander Goehr – Metamorphosis Dance, Romanza for Cello and Orchestra**
1990, Unicorn-Kanchana Records UKCD 2039
Goehr – Metamorphosis/Dance, Op. 36
Goehr – Romanza for Cello and Orchestra, Op. 24

**Alexander Goehr, Jeanine Thames, London Sinfonietta Conducted by Oliver Knussen – ... A Musical Offering (J.S.B. 1985) / Behold the Sun / Lyric Pieces / Sinfonia**
1991, Unicorn-Kanchana DKP(CD) 9102
Goehr – ... A Musical Offering, Op. 46
Goehr – Behold the Sun, Op. 44a
Goehr – Lyric Pieces, Op. 35
Goehr – Sinfonia, Op. 42

**Goehr* – Jacqueline du Pré, Daniel Barenboim, New Philharmonia Orchestra – Romanza for Cello and Orchestra / Symphony in One Movement**
1993, Intaglio INCD 7671
Goehr – Romanza, Op. 24
Goehr – Symphony in One Movement

**Goehr – The Death of Moses**
1993, Unicorn-Kanchana Records DKP(CD)9146
Goehr – The Death of Moses

**Wavesongs**
1994, NMC D019
Goehr – Cello Sonata, Op. 45

**Goehr: Piano Concerto**
1995, NMC D023
Goehr – Piano Concerto, Op. 33
Goehr – Symphony in One Movement, Op. 29

**Snapshots: Fiftieth Birthday Tributes for Oliver Knussen**
1996, London Sinfonietta SINF CD1-2004
Goehr – Only 2 Notes for Ollie

**Goehr: Arianna**
1998, NMC D054
Goehr – Arianna, Op. 58

**Hymnos**
1998, Clarinet Classics CC0019
Goehr – Paraphrase on Monteverdi's "Il combattimento di Tancredi e Clorinda", Op. 28

**Goehr & Carter: Chamber works**
2000, Cambria CAMCD-8804
Goehr – Five Objects Darkly, Op. 62

**Music of the Night**
2002, Scandinavian Classics 220556-205
Goehr – Nonomiȳa, Op. 27

**Alexander Goehr – Sing, Ariel**
2003, NMC D096
Goehr – Sing Ariel, Op. 51
Goehr – The Mouse Metamorphosed into a Maid, Op. 54
Goehr – The Death of Moses, Op. 53

**Alexander Goehr – Behold the Sun**
2003 , NMC D095
Goehr – Metamorphosis / Dance, Op. 36

Goehr – Romanza, Op. 24
Goehr – ... A Musical Offering, Op. 46
Goehr – Behold the Sun, Op. 44a
Goehr – Lyric Pieces, Op. 35
Goehr – Sinfonia, Op. 42

**Goehr · Hamilton – Violin Concertos**
2004, EMI Classics 7243 5 86189 2 1
Goehr – Violin Concerto, Op. 13

**Paul & Huw Watkins · British Cello Sonatas**
2004, Nimbus NI 5699
Goehr – Sonata, Op. 45

**On Christmas Day (New Carols From King's)**
2005, EMI Classics 7243 5 58070 2 1
Goehr – Carol for St. Steven

**Goehr: Symmetry Disorders Reach**
2007, Wergo WER66922
Goehr – Symmetry Disorders Reach

**Goehr – String Quartet No. 2**
2008, Lyrita SRCD264
Goehr – Little Symphony, Op. 15
Goehr – String Quartet No. 2, Op. 23
Goehr – Piano Trio, Op. 20

**Music by Alexander Goehr**
2008, Meridian Records CDE 84562
Goehr – Trio for Violin, Cello and Piano
Goehr – Suite for Violin and Piano
Goehr – Largamente, from Op. 18
Goehr – Piano Quintet

**Alexander Goehr**
2008, Lyrita SRCD.264
Goehr – Little Symphony
Goehr – String Quartet No. 2
Goehr – Piano Trio

**Il Combattimento di Tancredi e Clorinda**
2009, Flora 5425008377919
Goehr – Paraphrase on the Dramatic Madrigal "Il combattimento di Tancredi e Clorinda" by Monteverdi, Op. 28

**The NMC Song Book**
2009, NMC D150
Goehr – Ulysses' Admonition to Achilles

**Music for Solo Clarinet**
2010, Naxos 8.572470
Goehr – Paraphrase on the Dramatic Madrigal "Il combattimento di Tancredi e Clorinda" by Monteverdi, Op. 28

**Alexander Goehr: Colossos or Panic**
2012, NMC D165
Goehr – Colossos or Panic
Geohr – The Deluge, Op. 7
Goehr – Little Symphony, Op. 15

**Goehr: Piano Concerto**
2012, NMC D023
Goehr – Piano Concerto, Op. 33
Goehr – Symphony in 1 Movement, Op. 29

**Goehr: Marching to Carcassonne**
2013, Naxos 8573052
Goehr – When Adam Fell, Op. 89

Goehr – Pastorals, Op. 19
Goehr – Marching to Carcassonne, Op. 74

**Since Brass, nor Stone…**
2013, NMC D187
Goehr – Since Brass, nor Stone…, Op. 80
Goehr – … Around Stravinsky, Op. 72
Goehr – Clarinet Quintet, Op. 79
Goehr – Manere, Op. 81
Goehr – Largo Siciliano, Op. 91

**Choirbook for the Queen**
2013, Priory PRCD1097
Goehr – Cities and Thrones and Powers

**New Music Collections Vol. 1 – Choral**
2014, NMC D204
Goehr – The Death of Moses, Op. 53

**Chimes in Time: Panayiotis Demopoulos**
2014, Prima Facie PFCD013
Goehr – Nonomiȳa

**The Silken Tent**
2019, Signum SIGCD826
Three Sonnetts and Two Fantasias, Op. 68

**Anna Meredith: Triptotage Miniatures; Colin Matthews: Postludes; Alexander Goehr: After "The Waking"**
2020, NMC D239
Goehr – After "The Waking"

## FURTHER INFORMATION

### Alexander Goehr

https://www.schott-music.com/en/person/alexander-goehr#person_info_view

### Jack Van Zandt

https://www.jackvanzandt.com/
https://composersedition.com/jack-van-zandt/

Recordings of many of Goehr's works are available on Jack Van Zandt's YouTube Channel separately and in playlists: https://www.youtube.com/channel/UCAPa4s-KkuHvzsmh3wkLIug

**INDEX**

Adès, Thomas 22
Adorno, Theodor 96
Alberti, Rafael 27
Alldis, John 140
Anderson, Julian 22, 231
Aprahamian, Felix 60
Arnold, Irmgard 112
Arom, Simha and Sonia 32
Atherton, David 33, 103
Attwood, Thomas 70

Babbitt, Milton 14, 58–9, 63, 99, 102, 123, 132–3, 150, 153–5, 181, 192,
Babcock, David 22, 149
Bach, Carl Philipp Emanuel 26, 174, 176, 189–191
Bach, Johann Sebastian 71, 73, 114, 116, 136–145, 163–4, 167–9, 187–91, 216, 221, 242
Bachelard, Gaston 76
Backhaus, Wilhelm 56
Bacon, Francis 89
Balthus (Balthasar Kłossowski de Rola) 128
Barenboim, Daniel 119, 247
Bartók, Béla 23–4, 86, 88, 95, 97–8, 130, 155, 192
Bartolozzi, Bruno 121–2, 234
Beckett, Samuel 27
Beethoven, Ludwig van 33, 50, 70–1, 111, 113, 138, 140, 155, 163, 166–7, 169, 188, 228
Benjamin, George 22, 30
Berg, Alban 62, 66, 77, 97–8, 110, 114, 124, 181, 185
Berio, Luciano 25
Birtwistle, Harrison 1, 16, 28, 32, 52, 58–60, 64, 80, 94, 119–20, 153, 167, 180, 198, 218, 232
Bizet, Georges 216

253

Blake, David 111
Blake, William 200, 203, 245
Boulanger, Nadia 86
Boulez, Pierre 1, 14, 25, 29, 33, 60, 64, 68, 77, 80–93, 95–105, 108, 128, 154, 156, 168, 183, 192–3, 196, 219
Boult, Adrian 219
Boyde, Patrick 141
Brahms, Johannes 58, 87, 121, 156, 164, 169, 176, 207, 216, 219
Brandt, Bill 45
Brecht, Bertolt 106–7, 112–3, 115, 151, 201, 207–8
Brittain, Vera 50
Britten, Benjamin 109, 113, 156, 202–3, 207, 212
Brown, Earle 157
Burnby, Colin 22
Burnett, Jimmy and Janet 32
Busoni, Ferruccio 56–7, 61–2, 66, 83
Byrd, William 26, 63
Byron, George Gordon (Lord Byron) 61, 199

Cage, John 104–5, 152
Cardew, Cornelius 104
Carewe, John 84
Carr-Boyd, Ann 22
Carter, Elliott 25, 144, 149, 155–6, 248
Carter, Helen 192
Celan, Paul 209
Cézanne, Paul 164
Chen Yi 22
Chomsky, Noam 27
Chopin, Frédéric 87, 169, 176
Churchill, Winston 210
Claudel, Paul 76
Cleghorn, Arthur 44
Coltrane, John 198

Cone, Edward T. 150
Cook, Nicholas 22, 30
Copland, Aaron 109, 149
Couperin, François 26
Cowie, Edward 22, 226
Crumb, George 150

d'Indy, Vincent 87
Dallapiccola, Luigi 25, 93, 96, 98–9
Davies, Peter Maxwell 'Max' 1–2, 16, 28, 52, 58–60, 62, 64, 72, 83, 101, 115–6, 120, 144, 167, 180, 196, 205, 218, 232, 247
Debussy, Claude 25, 29, 74, 77, 89–90, 99, 156, 179, 218
Delius, Frederick 52, 54, 153
Demant, Charlotte 54, 127
Deutsch, Max 65, 67–8, 79
Disney, Walt 183
Dolphy, Eric 198
Dow, John 60
Dowland, John 211
Draper, Charles 120
Drew, David and Judy 32
du Pré, Jacqueline 119, 247
Dukas, Paul 76
Dunstable, John 26
Dushkin, Samuel 123

Eisenstein, Sergei 27, 203
Eisler, Georg 201
Eisler, Hanns 14, 42, 54, 81, 92, 106–118, 127, 181, 201, 207–8
Elinson, Iso 51–2, 58
Eliot, T.S. 48, 205–6
Ellington, Duke 217
Eluard, Paul 76
Emmanuel, Maurice 76

Fenlon, Iain 32
Feyerabend, Paul 194, 235
Forte, Alan 133
Frederick II of Prussia (the Great) 141
Fricker, Peter Racine 16, 20, 225
Fried, Erich 200–1
Froom, David 22, 149, 228

Gardiner, John Eliot 203, 219
Geehl, Henry 49
Gerhard, Roberto 42
Gershwin, George 157, 211
Gershwin, Ira 211
Giacometti, Alberto 128
Gibbons, Orlando 202
Gielen, Michael 30, 33
Gilbert, Anthony 22, 227
Gilliam, Laurence 44
Glock, William 61
Goehr, Julius 40–42
Goehr, Laelia 1, 39–40, 235
Goehr, Rudolph 42, 158
Goehr, Thekla 40
Goehr, Walter 1, 14, 16, 39–41, 46, 80–1, 106, 126, 214–15
Goethe, Johann Wolfgang 225
Goldstein, Rosa 43
Goya, Francisco 159, 167, 195, 238
Graebner, Eric 232
Grieg, Edvard 40
Groves, Sally 2, 10–11, 32
Guilini, Carlo Maria 140
Gurdjieff, George 52

Hacker, Alan 119–20, 198
Hall, Richard 1, 14, 48, 51–61, 64–5, 70, 81, 83, 127, 157, 177, 179–81, 192, 218, 220
Hamilton, Iain 227, 249
Handel, George Frideric 26, 115, 143, 164, 168–9, 217
Hannenheim, Norbert von 42
Hartog, Howard 61
Harvey, Jonathan 232
Hauer, Josef Matthias 56, 59
Haydn, Joseph 50, 87, 171
Hearn, Lafcadio 200
Henze, Hans Werner 96
Hesse, Hermann 27
Hill, first name unknown, Greek and Latin teacher 45–7
Hindemith, Paul 42, 44, 57, 78, 181, 218
Hitler, Adolf 1, 40, 54
Holloway, Robin 22, 32
Honegger, Arthur 77
Hopkins, Gerard Manley 209
Horowitz, Vladimir 40
Howarth, Elgar 'Gary' 28, 52, 60
Huang, Joan 22, 149, 229
Hudson, W.H. 203
Hull, Arthur Eaglefield 53
Huxley, Aldous 27

Isaac, Heinrich 168
Ives, Charles 25, 115, 156, 201–2

Janáček, Leoš 158, 200
Jeppeson, Knud 69
Jolivet, André 73, 76
Joyce, James 27

Kafka, Franz 27, 31, 199, 246
Kalmus, Alfred 51
Kandinsky, Wassily 27, 225
Kaper, Bronislaw 43
Katz, Amira 31
Kell, Reginald 44, 119
Keller, Hans 169, 232
Kermode, Frank 211–2
Kirnberger, Johan 190
Kirschner, Leon 157
Kitchin, Margaret 61
Klee, Paul 26, 96, 168, 193, 225, 231
Knussen, Oliver 33, 89, 128–30, 132, 152, 154, 221, 247–8
Kolisch, Rudolf 96
Kotoński, Włodzimierz 105
Krenek, Ernst 25, 56–9, 61, 155, 181

Lachmann, Robert 63
Landers, Joseph 149
Le Jeune, Claude 77
Leibowitz, René 84–5, 93, 95, 101,
Leskov, Nikolai 201
Ligeti, György 25
Liszt, Franz 61
Loos, Adolf 62
Loriod, Yvonne 14, 47, 60–1, 63–5, 68–70, 80, 83, 88, 96
Lutosławski, Witold 105
Lutyens, Elizabeth 61–2

Machaut, Guillaume de 216
Mackerras, Charles 201–2
Maderna, Bruno 93–6, 99-100
Mahler, Gustav 216
Mallarmé, Stéphane 91
Mann, Thomas 27, 114, 235

Martinet, Jean-Louis 84
Marx, Groucho 201, 206
Marx, Karl 76, 110
Matzerath, Otto 103
Meltzer, Harold 22, 149
Mendelssohn, Felix 113–4, 143
Messiaen, Olivier 1, 14, 25, 30, 58–68, 70–81, 83–5, 90, 95–98, 100, 102–3, 105, 122, 165, 180, 182–5, 189, 191, 232, 235, 242
Milhaud, Darius 62, 76–7, 95, 153
Milstein, Silvina 22, 235
Milton, John 200, 203, 208
Mirrlees, James 32
Mitropoulos, Dimitri 59
Mizler, Lorenz 143
Monteverdi, Claudio 71, 122, 136, 140–1, 163–4, 189, 194–8, 216, 219, 240, 248, 250
Mozart, Wolfgang Amadeus 50, 70–1, 73, 102, 104, 121, 125, 138, 163, 165, 168–9, 177, 188, 221
Musgrave, Thea 16, 20
Mussorgsky, Modest 77, 167, 179

Nancarrow, Conlon 156
Nigg, Serge 84
Nin, Anaïs 158
Nono, Luigi 1, 25, 68, 93–4, 96, 98, 100–1, 104, 158
Northcott, Bayan 22, 234

Ogdon, John 1, 28, 52, 60–2, 95, 180, 218, 241
Olivier, Laurence 206, 210
Orwell, George 27
Ouspensky, Pyotr 52
Ozawa, Seiji 158

Palestrina, Giovanni Pierluigi da 88, 98, 140, 194–5
Penderecki, Krzysztof 105
Petrassi, Goffredo 63

Petri, Egon 56
Picasso, Pablo 26, 167, 170, 195, 199
Piscator, Erwin 27, 42, 235
Pollini, Maurizio 32–3
Poole, Geoffrey 22, 232
Porter, Cole 211
Poulenc, Francis 77, 86
Pound, Ezra 211
Pousseur, Henri 68, 94–5, 100
Prausnitz, Frederik 151, 157
Pritchard, John 103
Prokofiev, Sergei 109, 203
Purcell, Henry 62, 101, 216

Rameau, Jean-Philippe 26, 189–90
Ravel, Maurice 77, 85, 159, 191, 218
Reger, Max 131, 219
Reizenstein, Franz 45
Réti, Rudolph 218
Richards, Emma-Ruth 22, 230
Riemann, Hugo 139, 218
Rilke, Rainer Maria 208–9
Rinuccini, Ottavio 135, 141
Rodgers, Richard 211
Rolfe, Frederick (Baron Corvo) 220
Rosé, Arnold 54, 127
Rosen, Charles 169, 235
Rosenman, Leonard 185
Rousseau, Henri 'Douanier' 73, 183
Rufer, Josef 181, 235
Ruskin, John 225

Sackman, Nicholas 22
Sartre, Jean-Paul 85
Scarlatti, Domenico 26

Schenker, Heinrich 71, 102, 218,
Scherchen, Hermann 100
Schillinger, Joseph 58, 156–7
Schoenberg, Arnold 1, 16, 25, 42, 44, 48, 54, 56–7, 59, 61–3, 67, 76, 78–9, 80, 84–5, 87, 89, 92, 95–99, 101, 103, 105–7, 109–10, 113, 124–134, 215–8, 149, 153, 155, 157, 181, 186, 194, 203, 207, 235–6
Schubert, Franz 85, 113, 169, 176, 207–8, 216, 238
Schuller, Gunther 152–4, 156–7, 198
Schumann, Robert 50, 87, 138, 163, 169, 207, 238
Schweitzer, Albert 144
Scriabin, Alexander 25, 53–4, 77, 186
Searle, Humphrey 61, 235
Sechter, Simon 102–3, 165
Seiber, Mátyás 45
Semegen, Daria 22, 149, 233
Serkin, Peter 119, 152, 168, 221
Sessions, Roger 149–51, 155, 177
Shakespeare, William 107, 199–200, 203, 208-210
Shapey, Ralph 151
Shelley, Percy Bysshe 140
Shostakovich, Dmitri 109, 171, 201
Siegele-Wenschkewitz, Leonore 138
Siegele, Ulrich 14, 136–45, 164, 167, 188, 194
Silverstein, Joe 157
Skalkottas, Nikos 42
Smalley, Roger 22
Spinner, Leopold 187
Stadlen, Peter 127
Stadler, Anton 121
Stein, Hedwig 58
Steinecke, Wolfgang 95
Steuermann, Eduard 96
Stockhausen, Karlheinz 59, 68, 78, 88, 94–5, 98, 100-1, 104, 193
Stravinsky, Igor 25, 44–5, 48, 56, 59, 76–7, 79, 84, 87, 95, 97–8, 123, 130–2, 152, 155, 169, 179, 184, 191, 215–6, 241, 251

Taverner, John 28
Theodorakis, Mikis 86
Tippett, Michael 2, 14, 45–6, 48, 50, 202–3, 219
Tremblay, Gilles 75
Tudor, David 104–5

Varèse, Edgard 25, 73, 84, 98, 158
Velázquez, Diego 167, 195
Villa-Lobos, Heitor 77, 153
Villon, François 110

Wagner, Richard 50, 71, 77, 87, 157
Ward, David 22
Webern, Anton 24–5, 29, 59, 84–5, 88–9, 95–7, 99–100, 103, 105, 110, 114, 122, 124, 130, 132, 138, 154, 166, 181, 186–7, 193, 203
Weill, Kurt 42, 112, 218
Weiss, Peter 201
Wigglesworth, Ryan 32
Wilder, Billy 43
Williams, Bernard 32
Wittgenstein, Ludwig 27, 90
Wollheim, Richard 164, 195
Wolpe, Stefan 92, 149, 151–2
Wood, Hugh 32

Xenakis, Iannis 25

Yeats, William Butler 48

Zhou Long 22
Zillig, Winfried 42
Zimmermann, Bernd Alois 94
Zinovieff, Peter 16, 32